Eric W. Robinson.
January 1967.

HERBERT L. McDONALD

photographs by the author

British Columbia:
Challenge in Abundance

published by
The Canadian Confederation Centennial Committee of British Columbia.

Jacket and front end paper: Long Beach, West Coast Vancouver Island

SPLENDOR SINE OCCASU

About this Book

WHAT IS BRITISH COLUMBIA? Is it man or child, tough or tender, tumultuous or tranquil? Is it sea or high country, lush forest or arid plateau, cool rain or dry heat, business suit or plaid shirt? Whatever it is, the Committee said, find it. Picture it, write it, gather it into a book of 160 pages. Show us what we're like after our first 100 years.

Twelve thousand miles later I know ten books could not reflect all the image, so vast, so magnificently vast, is our tumbled province — awesome, inspiring, infuriating, with a picture every mile and visual experiences every day that beggar description. It is a humbling land. Inadequacy replaces self-confidence as exploration continues. It is not possible to communicate it all. Fascinated, delving deep into the heartland, you ascend, descend, cross rivers, cling to the wall on a chasm's curve, slip along the grassland. You long for the sun in the forests, sweat under it in the dry hills. The people are open-handed and wonderful. You listen and you soak it up. You climb into the camper's upper bunk and listen to the creek outside or the rain on the metal roof or the rustle of a night animal or the boom as a chunk of glacier falls into the valley. You relive the day and then one night the right word comes: Abundance! . . . overflowing . . . more than enough . . . plentiful . . . affluent . . . Abundance is all these things. Mountains and prairie, rock and resources, scenery and scope, chance and challenge — it is all here. Challenge? You wonder. Where else on this continent does the chance remain for true challenge? Where else can men test their energy and ingenuity against a frontier so formidable? So the pattern emerged.

Thus this book is not a tourist's guide nor a factual compendium. It is not your home town, your favourite view, industry or leisure activity. It is all of these things and it is none of these things. It is, within the range of the still camera's lens and the limit of words, enough provocation I hope, to entice you to go see for yourself. See the Abundance! See the Challenges! If you are twenty be assured of an enviable future. If you are sixty, cry a little. At any age you will be uplifted, inspired, charged with excitement.

Ours is this kind of country.

H.L.M.

Canadian Confederation Centennial Committee of British Columbia

BOARD OF DIRECTORS
L. J. Wallace, Chairman
T. F. Orr   G. C. Hacker
W. E. Ireland   S. E. Hughes
E. F. Fox   Mrs. E. C. Wood
Honourable W. D. Black

PUBLICATIONS SUB-COMMITTEE
Seth Halton, Chairman
G. E. Bowes   H. P. McKeever
N. R. Hacking   B. Ramsey
G. L. Levy   E. G. Stroyan
A. Sutton

British Columbia:

Challenge in Abundance

Credits

A BOOK OF THIS KIND is never one man's effort. Without the co-operation of hundreds all over the province who gave guidance, information and hospitality, this book would not have been possible. The author thanks them. Special thanks are due Seth Halton, Harry McKeever and Willard Ireland for editorial assistance; the information officers of provincial departments and industries who produced latest figures; Justin de Goutiere, B.C. Airlines, who piloted the author 4,000 miles for the aerial photos; James Murphy, Okanagan Helicopters, for the metro Vancouver flying; Glen Hyatt of Evergreen Press whose enthusiasm made the task easier; the wonderful people who posed and the unsuspecting ones who didn't know. Thanks are due Hal Arnold, (sketches, pages 18-19); Department of Lands, Forests & Water Resources (bottom photo, page 36); Okanagan Helicopters (bottom left, page 88); Fips Broda (page 141); Dept. Recreation & Conservation (page 144); Julian Messner, Division of Simon & Schuster, Inc., for permission to quote (page 71) the extract from *The Book of the Seven Seas* . . . Most of all the author thanks L. J. Wallace and his Centennial Committee for leadership and faith.

The Author

Herbert L. McDonald, 52, was educated in Vancouver, enlisted in 1941 and in the 14 years after the war became well known in Montreal and Toronto as a commercial and industrial photographer, writer and graphic arts designer. He returned to British Columbia in 1959 to reside in West Vancouver.

SKILLED AND TOUGH, tree
faller George Merchison,
38, photographed in the
Queen Charlotte Islands,
typifies hard-hatted British Columbia today as it
begins its second century.

1

A Vast and Vital Land

If all the world's a stage, British Columbia is one of its most dramatic sets. It is an ice-capped, forest-floored, mineral-rich, water-blessed mountain domain. It is a land of abundance, opportunity and magnificence.

Untamed, restless and bold, the province is one of the last great frontiers in North America. It is a land for the young, for dreamers, doers and for those who still seek a challenging life. It is an impudent land, here cultivated, there wild, often benign, sometimes angry, always active. *Energetic* describes it best.

It is a land where a man can make a million or lose his shirt. Many have done both. In its founding days the symbolic sound of a boom was the clunk of gold nuggets; now it is the rustle of stock certificates. There are other sounds: chain saws whine, cables twang, machinery grinds, drills chatter and explosives blast the sanctuary of the wilderness.

Paradoxically it is a land of exquisite softness, jewel-like lakes, soliloquizing creeks and the dreamy whisper of sand sifting across the sage. The big bass of its orchestral symphony comes from the thunder of the Pacific surf; the tremolo is the tinkle of a chime-like ripple against a bush plane's float swinging to its mooring. In the cathedral groves, afloat on the sea, on the crags and against the broad sky of its rolling plains a man stands tall.

It is a land of sharp personal experiences, treasured, unforgettable, like the smell of the fog and the dirge of the fog horns. It is the experience of intense interior heat and the biting wind-chill, the call of an elk, the approach of a moose, the chatter of a Steller's jay and the snarl of a cougar. There are memories of the pungent sea-smell of clams boiling in the old beach pot, dry cedar crackling in the fireplace, a taut line screaming from the reel, the echo of a .30/30 along the timberline, the swissshh of skis and the bawling of white-faced Herefords on the open range.

A poet would call British Columbia a lyric in blank verse; a musician, a symphony by Sibelius; an aesthete, a redolence of sea and forest scents. To the retired it is peaceful; to the challengers, clamourous; to the sensitive, eye-filling. It is breath-taking to all.

It is not a lotus land of beauty alone. To harvest its riches means challenge, responsibility, work. British Columbians work hard. They play hard too, for they have that capacity.

Those who mine spend millions building townsites, punching roads, blasting off overburden in the form of glaciated granite armour. Those who log, assault tough territory, tough on men and tough on equipment. Those who fish commercially keep an ear cocked to the radio-telephone for gale warnings. Those who employ labour face skillful labour leaders. Those who build, build strong, for they never forget that while nature is pleasant today it can maul the disrespectful tomorrow. Those who explore, organize vehicles and equipment as they would a safari, for there are 366,255 square miles

to see and it is safe to say not one of its 1.9 million people has seen them all.

British Columbia is more than twice the size of Japan, more than three times the area of Italy. It is the United Kingdom, France and 41,000 square miles of Spain put together. It is Washington, Oregon, California and 36,500 square miles of Mexico. Occupying seventeen and a half degrees of latitude and eleven degrees of longitude, it is 365 air miles from Vancouver airport to the eastern boundary and 770 air miles to the northern border on the 60th parallel. The Queen Charlotte Islands are 850 miles farther west than San Francisco. Vancouver is 400 miles farther north than Toronto.

The topography is as varied as the geography is expansive. Since the surface influences the atmosphere above it, there may be as many types of weather in any one day as over most of Europe on the same day. At the same hour there can be fog at Prince Rupert, snow at Fort Nelson, rain at Vancouver, dry heat at Williams Lake in the Cariboo country and balmy sunshine at Victoria. On a day in March, it can be 49 above at Nanaimo and 29 below at Fort St. John. Two months later it may be 75 in the Fraser Valley and 95 in Quesnel, 250 air miles away. Along the mainland coast, depending on the location, the annual rainfall is 40 to 170 inches, while the Okanagan, a four-hour drive away, gets only 10 to 20 inches.

The precipitation is now regarded as a liquid harvest. It sustains the province's 7,000 square miles of fresh water and makes British Columbia the envy of many world areas which are concerned with the threat of drought. Holding more water than any other province or U.S. state, it produces 15.3 million kilowatt hours of electric power. It is a heritage among heritages.

That heritage produces another in the form of forest cover. Some 64 percent of Canada's trees of more than 10 inches in diameter at breast height, grow in British Columbia. The total forest land area is 214,000 square miles, twice the size of New Zealand. Commercial forests occupy 184,000 square miles, five times the size of Portugal. They contain 50 percent of Canada's standing timber and 93 percent of the land it grows on is under government control. When the 1.5 billion cubic feet of fir, hemlock, spruce, cedar and balsam is cut annually and converted into wood and paper products, it is valued at a billion dollars. In the mid-sixties, the province is producing 66 percent of Canada's lumber, 21 percent of its pulp, 13 percent of its paper and 82 percent of its softwood plywood.

It also produces almost half Canada's fishery for unlike the geography below the 49th parallel, where the entire U.S. seaboard lies unprotected from the Pacific combers, British Columbia has inherited 17,000 miles of treasured coastline. The spring, coho, pink, sockeye and chum salmon, halibut, cod, herring, whales, crabs, clams and shrimps taken from its waters each year approach $100 million in wholesale market value.

Third member of the triumvirate of treasure lies underground. The combined production of all mining is close to $300 million annually. Zinc is the principal contributor. There is lead, copper, molybdenum, iron, coal, gold, natural gas, petroleum products and industrial minerals, structural materials, fuels and metals. Mining has come a long way from the days when lonely men worked the creeks with gold pans and hand-rocked sluice boxes.

An industrial giant is springing from the heritages of trees, minerals, fish and water. In the mid-sixties, the leading secondary industries are sawmilling, pulp and paper, petroleum products, veneers and plywoods, fish products, dairying, meat packing, shipbuilding and repair, and industrial chemicals. A recent 15-year study indicates that the gross value of manufacturing has risen from $1.133 billion to $2.882 billion.

What of the people who drive this industrial machine? They are united in their zealous pride of land but they are too divided by geography, occupation, social conditions and race to be typed as yet. Where only a few years ago Indian, explorer and trapper trod, they are hacking at the mountains, tunnelling the massifs, bridging the rivers, taming the terrain, staking the valleys, building cities, forcing their determined way through the timber. Of many ethnic origins, they are combining Old World patience with New World techniques to build an empire that will be of lasting significance. In the process, many types are emerging.

In Vancouver and Victoria the British Columbian belongs to fine clubs. He is a patron of the symphony, opera, art, and theatre. He watches the stock exchange and his boat's performance with equal interest. He supports appeals for charity with generosity. He goes mad for football. He is a determined golfer and he spends a lot of time with the boys in the locker room. Nevertheless he is a family man at heart and his dearest possessions are those things associated with his family.

7

In Prince George, Kamloops, Kelowna and any number of smaller cities, he leads an informal life. He knows everyone and shares their trials and triumphs. He is a non-conformist, easy to meet, short on ceremony. He reads the big-city papers sometimes a day after publication and often he must travel a long way to see a medical specialist.

In the ranch country he is tall and lean, laconic and diffident, but when he has something to say he says it and it is usually worth hearing. He can look into the sun without sun glasses and his blue eyes are permanently framed in wrinkles. His house is probably built from peeled logs and its setting an artist's dream. The wide floor boards are hidden by cougar and bear pelts, mute reminders of predators that attacked his stock.

In the farming areas he has been quick to adopt new mechanical aids. His grain has won international awards for quality. He watches worriedly the migrations of ducks and Canada geese and bangs away when ducks linger too long on his fields.

THE LOVELY PACIFIC DOGWOOD

This is *cornus nuttallii*, Pacific Dogwood, the floral emblem of British Columbia. The official species grows on Vancouver Island, the adjacent coast and the lower Fraser Valley to 30 miles beyond Hope, below the 1,000-ft. level. Protected by law, its 4-6 petaled white blooms appear from April to June and sometimes again in September.

His freezer holds venison steaks and he is making room in it, he vows, for the next beaver to interfere with his stream. He is concerned with world conditions and he plans next year's crop with a gambler's hope. If he is an orchardist he is involved in insecticides, pesticides, miticides, herbicides and fungicides because the apricots, pears, plums, apples, peaches and grapes he grows have to support a large fruit export and canning industry.

And he may be almost an anachronism, a relic from history and a survivor of the founding breed. Remote in the forest vastness, he traps mink, weasel, marten, beaver and fox, trudging the circular trapline that takes him ten days to go around. Each night he beds down in one of his stopover cabins and his last thought is a prayer that the ice on the river will be thick enough when he crosses it tomorrow. Among the frozen trees and silent marshes he pursues a livelihood as old as man. In the rawest sense, nature supports him.

Thus, there is to be found in British Columbia almost the entire gamut of social structure and environment. A forest industry executive who travels province-wide must be equally as comfortable in his dinner jacket at a formal meeting in Vancouver one night as he will be in his bush clothes the next night having supper with a trading post family. There is a remarkable link between the two worlds and as time passes an understanding is growing in each of the other and of their importance to one another. One produces the raw materials, the other sells them. One is taming the frontier, the other is attempting to expand his firm's market. Each is dependent on the other.

Helping them both are the captains of industry, members of government departments, educators, science researchers, thinkers, creators, long-range planners. Oceanographers are studying the habits of the native fish. Silviculturists are delving into a fascinating world of wood fibres and their chemical content. Geologists are donning the seven-league boots of electro-mechanical exploration. Road engineers are tackling areas once thought impassable. Pilots are putting their aircraft into the most remote regions. In short, British Columbia is experiencing an unprecedented surge of development in which people are now ahead of planners in what they feel can be achieved.

What has been accomplished? That is the theme of this book. Only 100 years ago the land was given a name. Only in more recent years its biceps began to bulge. The British Columbian is no longer a hewer of wood and a drawer of water. Now he is an engineer of timber resources and a producer of hydroelectric power. While he cherishes his resources he knows they are needed by a resource-hungry world. This book attempts to show how he is meeting his responsibilities to himself, his customers and his treasure house.

The book attempts as well to indicate some of the challenges inherent in the abundance. There is the challenge flung by the pioneers, miners, railroaders and builders who with only axe and muscle power began the awesome job of making sense of one of the world's most jumbled examples of geography. There are new challenges every day.

Destiny has proffered its generous hand to British Columbia. At this time in history it is fitting to examine the kind of clasp destiny has been offered in return.

BRITISH COLUMBIA'S HISTORY began at the site of the Nootka Light (left) in 1774 when white men first landed on the west coast of Vancouver Island. Today, only 25 miles inland at the top of Tahsis Inlet, industry bustles with the loading (right) of structural lumber between decks of Greek freighter bound for London. The Greek is a former wartime Liberty ship.

The Giant Sleeps No Longer

For centuries the gargantuan land that was to become British Columbia lay slumbering in time. Today, bursting with vigour, it has acquired the personality of a composite giant who strides with goal and purpose. He is creating achievement each time he moves. He is pumping up the oil, growing grain and belching gas in the Peace. He is bulging the fish nets along the coast. He is irrigating the dry interior hills and bringing forth the produce. He is cutting the tall timber at the bases of the mountains while baring their tops for the ore inside. He is fattening the beef stock on the Chilcotin ranges, building fine homes, pursuing the arts and withal, remembering to have some fun. He is awake.

WHITE-FACED HEREFORDS graze over a summer range of the Diamond S Ranch high on Pavilion Mountain north of Lill

GRAY-GREEN ASBESTOS ORE to the amount of 743,700 tons was taken in 1965 from this 6,000-ft. level of the Cassiar Range, 45 miles south of the Yukon border.

PETROLEUM EXPLORATION drill rig crew adds another stand of pipe in Buick Creek area, north of Fort St. John. Such B.C. drilling in 1965 totalled 209 miles.

...jority of Cariboo grass-fed beef is "government choice"

FISH POUR IN SILVER FLOOD out of a fog-bound Pacific on to the grading decks of the modern processing plants strung along the length of the long coastline.

AGRICULTURE as practised in the dry hills near Ashcroft needs water distributed by such modern methods as this efficient wheel-moving irrigation system.

FUN IN THE SUN, a high art in B.C., is exemplified by these racing yachts gathered in Victoria's inner harbour for the start of the Swiftsure race the next day.

EDUCATION (right) accounts for largest portion of the provincial budget as more and more British Columbians seek specialized learning in arts and sciences.

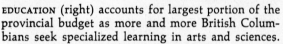

PRIDE OF OWNERSHIP in homes and gardens is a hallmark of provincial life. Apartment living is becoming increasingly popular but beautiful gardens remain.

THE REWARDS OF FAITH and hard work are all around in the works of God and man. Deep is the devotion in such a land — as here in New Denver on Slocan Lake.

REMAINS OF THREE TRADING POSTS, photographed in the summer of 1965, are some of many reminders that British Columbia's past is not so long ago. Top, Fort McLeod, first west of the Rockies, founded by Fraser, 1805. Centre, Fort Grahame, on the Finlay River, trading post of 1890. Bottom, Fort St. James, on Stuart Lake, the capital of New Caledonia, by Fraser in 1806.

2

From a Rugged Heritage

The Chinese claim to have discovered north-western America at the end of the fifth century. It is an indefinite claim unsupported by conclusive documents. The first true claim must be credited to Sir Francis Drake. In 1579 he departed the coast of Chile in search of a north-west passage. He named the northwest coast New Albion.

Some 160 years later, about 1741, Spain claimed the entire Pacific coast of America. In 1774 Juan Perez was commanded to sail north and take possession of the continent south of the posts that Russia had begun to establish. In July, from the deck of the *Santiago*, Perez first saw Nootka Sound and the Queen Charlotte Islands.

Other Spanish expeditions followed him. There are records of some trading with the Indians but none of an actual landing.

Then, in 1778, the Royal Navy's Captain James Cook came over the western horizon from the Sandwich Islands, with two ships, *Resolution* and *Discovery*. He landed at Nootka to become the first white man to set foot on the territory.

The arbitrary Spanish claims were challenged in the years that followed by traders of many nations seeking sea otter pelts. When British Captain Meares' ships were seized, England and Spain almost went to war. Peace prevailed with the signing of the Nootka Convention of 1790, when Spain relinquished her claim to the northwest coast. To enforce the treaty the Royal Navy's Captain George Vancouver arrived at Nootka in 1792. For three years his *Discovery* and *Chatham* navigated the intricate coastal waters, mapping and surveying.

The next principal in the drama was the North West Company which had been pushing its fur trade operations westward across the prairies. In the spring of 1793, that company's Alexander Mackenzie and nine companions followed the Peace River into the forbidding region west of the Rocky Mountains. They became the first white men to cross the continent overland when, on July 22, they reached salt water at Bella Coola on Bentinck Arm.

Mackenzie was followed by other

North West Company colleagues, Simon Fraser and David Thompson. Their discoveries and the trading posts they established produced an era of rivalry with the Hudson's Bay Company which had also moved into the area. In 1821 the North West Company was absorbed by the HBC and the latter became a catalyst in the development of British Columbia.

The territory west of the Rocky Mountains in which they had been operating was occupied jointly by England and the United States. That arrangement ended in 1846 when the 49th parallel and "the middle of the channel which separates the continent and Vancouver Island" were made the international boundary.

To buttress British rights, Vancouver Island was made a Crown Colony in 1849 and Richard Blanshard was commissioned to be the Crown's first representative. He requested his recall a few months later and was succeeded by the Hudson's Bay Company's chief officer, James Douglas. In 1853 his territory was enlarged to include the Queen Charlotte Islands because gold discoveries there had attracted American miners and British sovereignty again needed to be bolstered.

Over on the mainland, progress was slow. This changed suddenly when word leaked to San Francisco of gold discoveries on the Fraser River sandbars. The four

THESE WERE SOME OF THE PATHFINDERS. Left to right, below: Capt. James Cook, in 1778 became first white man to set foot on British Columbia; Capt. George Vancouver, in 1790 led British expedition to survey the coast; Bodega y Quadra, in 1792 was Spanish governor at Nootka; Sir Alexander Mackenzie, in 1793 was first white explorer to traverse continent north of Mexico; Simon Fraser, in 1808 explored the Fraser River for North West Company; Sir James Douglas, in 1843 founded Fort Victoria, is now called the "Father of British Columbia"; Richard Blanshard, in 1850 became the first Governor of Vancouver Island; Col. Richard Moody, Royal Engineers, in 1858 chose site of New Westminster as mainland capital, engineered the Cariboo road; Sir Matthew Begbie, in 1858 first judge on the mainland; John McCreight, in 1871 became the first premier after Confederation.

Capt. James Cook   Capt. George Vancouver   Bodega y Quadra   Sir Alexander Mackenzie   Simon Fraser

summer months of 1858 saw 20,000 gold-seekers arrive from California. To bring some control to the scene the British government established the mainland colony of British Columbia in August, 1858, and Douglas was made governor of this as well. The new colony was born formally at Fort Langley, November 19, 1858.

The gold fever spread. Miners pushed their frenzied search so far that by 1862 they were beyond the northern boundary of the colony. Again to ensure British possession, a fourth colonial jurisdiction was created, the Territory of Stickeen, and Douglas was handed its administration. A year later the boundaries of the mainland colony were enlarged to include the whole of the territory that is now mainland British Columbia.

For a time the two colonies, island and mainland, operated separately. With the gradual collapse of the gold excitement it became evident their individual existence was not efficient. Thus it was that on November 19, 1866, they were united and British Columbia was born. New Westminster on the Fraser River became the capital but on May 25, 1868, Victoria was named the seat of government.

The Dominion of Canada was formed July 1, 1867. When a railway was promised as an east-west link, British Columbia joined the Confederation on July 20, 1871. The following month Joseph Trutch became the province's first lieutenant-governor. He selected a lawyer, John Foster McCreight, to be the first premier and to form the first government.

In 1866 Victoria had been Queen 29 years. The Crimean War had ended 12 years before. Pasteur had just proven his theory of pasteurization. Dickens had written 15 books. The world outside was moving but the British Columbia story was just beginning.

The historic objects and the examples of Indian craft pictured on the next two pages are some of hundreds of such items stored in the Archives and Museum, Parliament Buildings, Victoria. They will be part of the fine collections in the Centennial Archives and Museum, now under construction in the capital city.

Sir James Douglas   Richard Blanshard   Col. Richard Moody   Sir Matthew Begbie   John F. McCreight

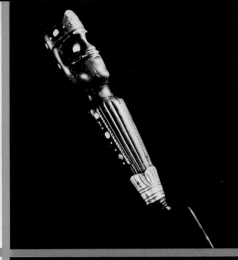

Above, carved sternpiece of Hudson's Bay Co. crest thought to be from *S. S. Beaver*. First below, ceremonial trumpet and helmet of Victoria Volunteer Fire Company in 1880's. Bottom, hat and hatbox belonging to Simon Fraser and brought to B.C. in 1864 by his son John who died at Barkerville, 1865.

Above, dagger believed used by the assassin of Capt. Cook at Kealakekua Bay, Hawaii, 1779. First below, original cross from church of St. John the Divine, Yale, 1860. Bottom, leather fire bucket from Barkerville, 1862, and a magic lantern with two original slides said to have been used as entertainment by miners.

Top above, cannibal bird mask used by dancers in Kwakiutl winter ceremonies. Above, Haida grease dish collected on the Queen Charlottes, 1889. Bottom, a "copper" of the Haidas of Skidegate on the Queen Charlottes. The heavy etched coppers were distinguishing marks of wealth and were highly prized.

Above, gavel used at opening of Parliament Buildings, 1898, and red sash worn over his coat by Sir James Douglas. First below, theodolite used in 1851 to survey townsite of Victoria. Bottom, flintlock gun of 1868 used by Hudson's Bay Co. in trade with Indians. Medicine kit was issued by the company to its fur traders.

Top above, fine examples of meticulous beadwork cradle boards by Kootenay Indians. Above, argillite Haida chest carved by one of the greatest Haida carvers, Charles Edensaw. Bottom, a Tsimshian chief's wooden headdress inlaid with abalone shell and painted red, black and blue. Sea lion whiskers stand on top.

Top above, Tlaoacha wooden mask of Kwakiutls with copper eyebrows, collected at Bella Bella, 1893. Above, spruce root hats of Haida design with mountain goat wool Chilkat blanket of Tsimshians. Bottom, canoe figurehead attributed to Haida, although decorated prows like this are considered typical of Tlingit.

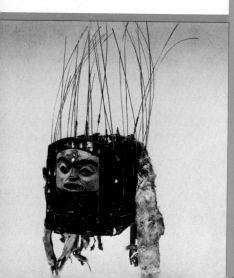

Not So Very Long Ago

In 1866, when British Columbia became an entity, Henry Fox Talbot's invention of the camera was 10 years old. For this reason today's British Columbians, unlike people of other, older places, can relive their first century in photographs without relying on the artistic licence of artists. The fact that the past can be relived in photographs, be they ever so antique and time-worn, seems to shorten the intervening years and makes the past not so very long ago. One of the interesting aspects of the Parliament Buildings in Victoria is the opportunity to come face to face with history through the collections of memorabilia on display. In the Provincial Archives' filing cabinets, row on row, is a treasure of prints from glass plate negatives. They represent almost every area of the province. In the collection are found the wanderers, builders, plunderers, challengers, their work, habits, homes and tribulations. Here are some of those photographs. They provide a unique and graphic portrayal of a life that is still in living memory of many of the province's older citizens. Nobody smiles in the photographs, a characteristic of the stiff pose required for the long, lens-cap-off, lens-cap-on exposure demanded by the slow emulsion.

VICTORIA FIRE DEPARTMENT of 1890 (above) poses during a practice run at corner of Johnson and Douglas streets. The population of the city then was 22,500.

QUEUEING FOR KLONDIKE PERMITS (below) gold-seekers crowd Victoria Customs House steps in 1898. Permits cost $10. Building is now used as an enlistment centre.

14-FT. DIAMETER FIR lay at site of Vancouver's Georgia and Seymour intersection in 1885. Part of this log was shown at London's Colonial Exhibition in 1887.

BRIDGE TO STANLEY PARK, Vancouver, thought to be in 1898. Event not known. It collapsed in 1905, was repaired, then replaced by present causeway in 1917.

FLOOD AND FIRE struck many new townsites. Above, Kaslo, 1894, when creek rose 33 feet above low water. Below, Rossland, 1902, when four blocks were razed.

CHESLATTA LAKE CHIEF and family, (below) in 1926, at Ootsa Lake, southwest of Fort Fraser. Belonging to Carrier tribe, chief held sway over rich hunting area.

OXEN-PULLED FREIGHT WAGONS in 1882 at Boston Bar on the Cariboo Road. The wagons averaged four to 12 miles a day to the gold fields. Freight cost $1 a pound.

QUESNELMOUTH IN 1885, at the junction of the Fraser and Quesnel rivers, now Quesnel. Bank of B.C. is 2nd cabin from right. There were 200 whites and Chinese.

WHITE'S PALACE SALOON of the Nelson Hotel, (above) was at the time of this photo, 1897-1900, gathering place for miners in the great mining boom of the era.

PIONEERS OF YALE pose on the saloon porch in 1867. Below, Columbia Street, New Westminster, Sunday, Sept. 11, 1898, after 60-block fire during the night.

PRINCE RUPERT in 1910. The Grand Trunk Pacific was laying rail to the east. The population was 3,000. Some 25 land firms were touting lots up to $6,000.

HAGWILGET BRIDGE over Bulkley River, in 1900, built by Indians of poles and wire left by Overland Telegraph. Below, a streetcar on Baker Street, Nelson, in 1905.

STEAM LOGGING on Vancouver Island was practised until World War II. This photo was taken about 1917. The locomotive is a Climax, replaced later by a Shay.

S.S. BEAVER, first steamer on north Pacific, in 1888, same year she was wrecked. Below, Barkerville miners taken by F. Dally, early B.C. photographer, in 1867.

INDIAN BRASS BAND at Sechelt during dedication of Oblate Church, 1890. There were many such bands. In 1905, New Westminster Fair had seven competing.

NEVERSWEAT

FORT STEELE in the Kootenays is presently being restored by the provincial government into a typical mining town of the period as an historical attraction.

GHOST TOWN OF SANDON, Slocan country's silver capital, incorporated 1892, had 24 hotels, 23 saloons. Derelict buildings were smashed in the flood of 1955.

MINERS' MOSSY BOOKS, old boots (left) with pack rats are all that remain in the famous Premier gold mine's crumbling mountainside dormitory north of Stewart.

RESTORATION OF BARKERVILLE, begun in 1958, progresses yearly. Working from plans and an original photo, carpenters begin to reconstruct Assay Office.

3

Nature is Dominant

In terms of contemporary history British Columbia is a youngster. In the geological pedigree of the world it is a venerable patriarch dating back to the Pre-Cambrian era, 650 million years ago. In the Jurassic period, 180 million years ago, the present area of the province was under the sea and there was a land mass west of the present coastline now called Cascadia. Then, 130 million years ago, eruptions raised the present coastal mountains and the Columbia system far to the east. The Cretaceous period, 100 million years ago, was one of great erosion. It in turn was followed by the tremendous movements of the earth's crust which formed the Rocky Mountains 65 million years ago. The Miocene period, 25 million years ago, brought the sinking of Cascadia and left only the tops of the higher mountains to form what is now Vancouver Island, the Queen Charlotte Islands and smaller offshore islands. Volcanic outpourings left great depths of lava over much of the southern interior and the Columbia basin.

This was followed by the Pleistocene period of a million years ago when the entire area of what is now the province was covered with a sheet of ice extending 100 miles into the present state of Washington. It began its retreat only 30,000 years ago and in the process formed the province's present topography. The advancing ice had gouged the valleys, produced the peaks and indented the coast with fiords. The loose material it had shovelled up had been left at the bottoms of the large lakes formed temporarily by the melting ice. Wind and water are still sculpting the face of British Columbia. Great rivers like the Fraser, whose delta is home to almost half the provincial population, are still carving into the valleys and still depositing their alluvium at their mouths.

The geological history of the province has not yet been charted completely but certain fascinating details are known. It has been determined that at its maximum the ice blanket was more than 8,000 feet thick over the southern interior and that its weight at one time depressed the Fraser River delta 1,000 feet. The last volcanic eruption in the provincial area was only about 300 years ago. Once there was 575 feet of sea water over the site of Vancouver. Today, 75 percent of the province is 3,000 feet above sea level.

The shaping and re-shaping left British Columbia with eleven distinct physiographic divisions within four separate systems. In the western mountain system there are the insular mountains, the coastal trench and the coast mountains. Making up the interior plateau system are the Fraser and Nechako plateaus and the northern plateau. The eastern mountain system combines the Cassiar and Omineca mountains, the mountains of the Columbia, the Rocky Mountains and a geological freak, the Rocky Mountain Trench. The interior plains system comprises the Peace River basin and the Fort Nelson River basin.

Each division of each system is almost another world, another country. One is rich in minerals, another is almost sterile. One is heavy with vegetation, another is desert. Tree growth is a good example of this. Two-hundred-foot-high spruce, six feet through at the stump, grow only feet apart on the Queen Charlottes. On the benches of the Thompson River in the dry

STATION "PAPA"

This is the new weathership *C.C.G.S. Vancouver* which began duty at Weather Station "Papa," September 1966, out in the Pacific, 670 miles due west of the north tip of Vancouver Island. Patrolling a 15-square-mile area at that position, it operates on station six weeks at a time radioing weather reports to Pacific Weather Central offices, Vancouver. When back for revictualling its place is taken by one of the now outdated converted frigates that have done yeoman service for so long. In March 1967, it will be joined by the *Quadra*, a similar $11 million vessel. Both were built by Burrard Drydock Co. Ltd., North Vancouver, for Dept. of Transport, Ottawa.

interior, eighty-foot-high ponderosa pine, two feet at the stump, regulate their population by the amount of moisture in the ground and grow sixty feet apart.

There are ten types of forest regions in Canada. Few provinces have more than two. British Columbia has seven. It also has nine zones of vegetation and many trees, shrubs and flowers are indigenous to only one. Over 3,000 forms of botanical life have been catalogued so far and new ones are discovered every year.

W eather, to a large extent the result of the topography, is another important factor in the way of life of the province. The Pacific Ocean is ringed by high mountains. The North American section of the ring is called the Cordilleran system. Since the weather moves from west to east in the temperate zones, the Cordillera forms a fantastic barrier to the main stream of the westerlies. As the moisture-laden low-pressure areas march in their seeming regularity upon the coast, the mountains force them into a higher, colder atmosphere and they drop their loads as rain or snow. The leeward side of the Coast range consequently is very dry. The storms are forced even higher over the Rockies than they were over the coast ranges but on their leeward side precipitation appears again. Thus, Ocean Falls on the coast of the mainland receives 170 inches of rain and Penticton in the Okanagan gets only 10 inches. Fernie, further east near the Alberta border, can count on 40 inches.

That the Cordillera in British Columbia, rising sharply from the sea, is a fortunate circumstance, is illustrated by comparison with the situation in Southern California where the higher mountains are 550 miles from the sea. There the water table of the Sacramento Valley is terrifyingly low compared to British Columbia which has five big drainages: the Yukon, Mackenzie, Fraser and Columbia river systems and the ten lesser rivers making up the coastal system. The *average* flow of their runoff to the sea is 133 trillion gallons a year!

The government weather forecasters are important men in British Columbia. In this era of pre-planning their advice is sought constantly. Despite the peculiarities of the region they are about 80 percent accurate. Their job is a tough one because the Department of Transport's western weather office has only two weather ships, with one on duty, at Station "Papa," 600 miles to the west of Vancouver Island. It has a very wide ocean to cover and few ships making regular, voluntary weather reports from scattered positions. In contrast, the United Kingdom forecasters depend on the reports of 11 weather ships around the domain, a smaller ocean to the west and many more ships reporting weather conditions on the crowded Atlantic sea-routes.

It is expected that with four ESSA weather satellites in polar orbit, both industry and public will be able to plan ahead with greater certainty. The ESSA satellites photograph 1,000 square miles at a time. Individual stations, like Pacific Weather Central at Vancouver, using a tracking receiver, will be able to bring the pictures to earth on command as the satellite passes overhead. More accurate, longer-ranged forecasting will be a welcome asset to the lumbering and fishing company planners, to the bush-plane pilots, to road construction engineers and most significantly to Forest Service fire protection men.

Diametrically opposed geographic and climatic characteristics breed people in regionally-oriented groups and for this reason, British Columbia is full of groups. An understandable insularity divides them. People who live on the humid, lush coast cannot have much in common with those who live in the dry, sparse interior. There are different sets of problems, different outlooks, different attitudes. Fortunately the dynamic pace of the mid-sixties is gradually correcting the condition and is tending to solidify the people of the province. So many engineers, executives of expanding industries, machinery operators and construction men are now deep into a hinterland which formerly had little contact with larger centres, that a better awareness is growing of regional problems and motivations. The huge construction jobs at the Peace and Columbia river damsites have been magnets drawing thousands out of the lower mainland and southern Vancouver Island area into the interior just to sight-see, a majority perhaps for the first time. Better, all-weather highways that no longer play second fiddle to the terrain but boldly strike out and maintain their direction, have made it easier for people-to-people and community-to-community contact.

Despite these advances however, there will always be the geographic and climatic differences. Not until they are fully understood can British Columbia and its people be appreciated. They are an agglomerate people in an agglomerate land that is uniquely complex. To develop it economically, to maintain the balance of nature and man, requires the wisdom of a Solomon, the dash of a frontiersman, the imagination of an engineer, the money of a Midas and the soul of a true visionary.

The Land Assumes Many Faces

It would take a much larger book to show all the faces of British Columbia. Here there is room for only four of the most basic: the peaks, the plains, the sea-girt coast and the coastal trough. A more complete list would include the twisted fiords of Rivers Inlet, the sparse hills of Kamloops, the finger lakes of the Kootenays, the tumbling waterfalls of Wells Gray Park, the ice fields of the Iskut, the straight white beaches of the Queen Charlotte Islands, the soft yellow hills of the Cariboo, the craggy canyons and utterly lonesome valleys of the Kechika and Finlay rivers, the Scottish landscape quality of Stuart Lake, the rocks and Garry oaks of the shore near Victoria, the mountain meadows of Garibaldi Park, the coral-coloured lakes set like opals in the forest floor, and that view of views – a Pacific sunset!

FERTILE FARMLAND of the Peace River grows wheat above its rich surface; holds great oil and gas deposits below it. This is the flat aspect of British Columbia.

THE PEAKS OF THE ROCKIES, below, form the rugged, white-browed face of the province. Only one hour's flying and 130 air miles separate the two photographs.

WHERE THE LAND CLIMBS OUT OF THE SEA on the far west coast of Vancouver Island, lush, furry fingers of green forest make gradual ascent to the range just beyond.

EAST OF THE COAST RANGE, 200 miles from the scene above, the face of the land is wrinkled and scarred with erosion as here on the course of the Fraser River.

The Many Moods of Weather

PERMANENTLY BENT TO THE PACIFIC WIND, trees of lonesome Long Beach on Vancouver Island's west coast assume slanted cluster shapes against the ocean's broad horizon, while against their rock bases, winds and breakers deposit a collection of sea-sweepings fascinating in diversity, texture and sculptured form.

WHEN MOUNTAIN STORMS gallop through the passes and scud across the peaks, their boiling grey mantles ride the wind in savage fury of sound and lashing rain. When they pass, the forests seem newly green, the slopes resound with birdsong.

THE RAIN FORESTS of coastal British Columbia are as dense as a jungle. Underbrush grows man-high in a year, surrounding the tall timber with lush growth.

WOOLLY FINGERS OF FOG OOZE up the coastal inlets from the ocean making isolated islands of mountain tops to create from high above, a scene of heavenly serenity.

WHITE RAIN in quantity is an occasional trial on the coast when a wintry Pacific low stalls in its eastward passage and coincides with a drop in the temperature.

4

Expansion
Fuelled by Natural Riches

Explore, exploit, export! Those three words might well form a new corporation symbol to depict the natural resources story of British Columbia in the mid-sixties.

The caulk-booted, plaid-shirted, virile-bearded group surrounding the rare rib steaks at the round table by the window of the upcountry Chinese cafe may look like bush rats but there are two B.Sc.'s, three M.Sc.'s and two Ph.D.'s among them. The remaining two will graduate next year. Their rock-dented Land Rovers are outside. Their helicopters are in a clearing a couple of blocks away. They are today's explorers and their number is legion. They work for a variety of companies and government departments. Some are geologists. Some are foresters. Nearly all are engineers of one kind or another. They are the moulders who are shaping the inherited natural geography into human and economic geography. They are a determined breed. Backed by enormous amounts of public and private capital, they are designing ways to go through and around mountains, to divert and dam rivers, to irrigate arid soil, to adjust the economy to the physical abundance of the rocks, soil, forests, rivers, the wild game of the land and the silver fish of the sea. If any one of them were told he was starring in a cinerama epic, as indeed he is, he would deny it. Nevertheless he is a trail blazer.

The blue-jeaned girl, arms around her knees, sits in the door of her long trailer home. She is dappled by sun and shadow filtering through the pines of the trailer court. The girl on the next trailer pad is hanging diapers. Two pads over, another is having her propane tank re-filled. They are legion too. Thousands like them are found in trailer communities on the edges of almost every population centre in the province, and in countless outposts. Their men are the exploiters of the natural wealth. Their job is to get it out. They could be hard-rock miners, power shovel operators, tree fallers, any one of a hundred specialized experts. They are hard and competent, highly trained, at one with their equipment. In contrast to pre-war days they now work to rigid controls set by their companies, complying with other strict controls set by the provincial government in the interests of conservation and resources management.

Providing direction and motivation is another luncheon group. It consists of market planners, production co-ordinators, vice-presidents of export sales. The conversation concerns market demand, labour demand, new sources of raw materials and the next quarterly report to shareholders of their companies. From their white-linened table by the club window framing a view of Vancouver harbour they watch a 35,000-tonner loaded to the plimsoll slip slowly out, bound for the docks of London. A few minutes later another goes by with ore for Osaka. Before lunch breaks up there will be a third ship with fish for Le Havre. They pay little heed. The cargoes the ships are carrying are the work of yesterday. Their job today is to plan the cargoes of tomorrow's ships. *Tomorrow* is one of their key words.

The verdant valleys and mountain slopes of British Columbia are really not green. Colour them gold. One way or another the forest products industry accounts for some 50 cents of every provincial income dollar. It is the largest enterprise in the province and not even dedicated citizens seem to fully appreciate all the startling facts. Here are some of the principal ones:

1) 58 percent of the province, 136.7 million acres, is forest land. Of this, 118 million acres sustain timber of commercial value. 2) The interior forest area east of the coast mountains is 103.2 million acres. This is seven times larger than the coast forest area with 14.8 million acres. 3) The provincial government controls more than 93 percent of the forest land; private owners administer five percent and the federal government controls the rest. 4) The annual loss of timber by decay alone is 600 million board feet, enough to build 60,000 average homes. 5) Forest industry workers total 12 percent of the provincial labour force and there are 50,000 trade union members among them. 6) The forest industry payroll totals $425 million a year. 7) About 30 percent of the provincial government's budget revenue is derived from the forests. 8) About 9 percent of Canada's foreign exchange comes from forest products originating in British Columbia. 9) The industry spends $3 million every working day for new plants, repairs, raw materials and manufacturing. 10) In 1966 there were more than 10,000 large and small logging operations, 1200 sawmills, 60 shingle mills, 25 veneer and plywood mills and 17 pulp and paper mills. Seventeen more pulp mills are being planned or are under construction.

There are some 4,000 companies engaged in logging and the manufacture of forest products. Of the half-dozen titans, the largest is MacMillan Bloedel Ltd. with annual sales of $430 million and net profit after taxes of $40 million. It harvests 1.5 billion board feet annually; sells a billion board feet as lumber, enough plywood ($^3/8$-in. basis) to cover 10.5 square miles. It manufactures some 1,000,000 annual tons of paper of all kinds. Its direct payroll is over $100 million a year for over 15,000 employees. A new $23 million newsprint machine at Port Alberni, one of the world's largest, produces 526 tons in 24 hours, the world's fastest. The company has begun operations in Holland, Spain, England and the United States.

A century ago, in 1865, 30 million board feet of lumber left coast mills by ship for export. In 1965, almost 2.5 billion board feet were exported, water-borne, some of it in superfreighters carrying more than twice 1865's entire output. The whole industry has changed. No longer does the faller's cry "Timberrr!" echo in the cutting area. He works alone now with one small, gasoline-driven chain saw and with it he downs a tree in a half hour that would have taken two men with a crosscut saw almost a day to fall prior to 1950. The Bunyanesque tree-topper is on the ground for good, his place taken by the mobile, telescoping steel spar. The stubby Shay logging locomotives and narrow-gauge logging railroads have been replaced by 100-ton diesel trucks and hundreds of miles of logging roads. Not many log booms are seen on the salt water coastline any more. They were slow to haul, subject to break up in storms and the teredo boring worm had the chance to munch his way through $2.5 million of logs a year. Now unique barges, nearly the size of football fields, carry logs to sawmills dumping automatically when they get there. A whole new technique has been adopted by the industry in the past decade.

The old, wasteful, cut-and-get-out practice has been replaced by sustained yield forestry which is based on the principle that annual harvest is regulated to annual growth. Administering this policy is the British Columbia Forest Service formed in 1912. It is now among the world leaders in the practice of sustained yield forestry and maximum utilization. It issues three main types of forest tenure.

One is called a tree farm licence. It is designed to enable private interests to practice sustained yield forestry. A logging outfit may acquire Crown timber for the usual fees to enlarge its operation then pledges to manage it according to Forest Service policy with respect to fire protection, annual cut and reforestation. The second type is called a public sustained yield unit. It is Crown land actually managed by the Forest Service, which disposes of the standing timber by sale to private operators. Harvest plans on such units are prepared by government foresters. The third and newest type of forest tenure is called a pulpwood harvesting area. It licences a pulp manufacturer to harvest small wood from forests already committed for sawlog purposes. Rather than replace a sawlog economy with a pulpwood economy it superimposes the latter on the former and everybody benefits. It is a practical application of the policy that no wood should be wasted.

Sustained yield forestry has brought new and significant stability to the industry. Improved extracting techniques which recover more than 70 percent of a tree, instead of the former 30 percent, plus an ever-growing market, have resulted in a constant and phenomenal growth in production values. Sawdust is an illustration of full utilization. Once it was discarded to stand out like an unsightly monument, or haze the valleys with its burning, or pollute rivers. Now it is used in the manufacture of pressed domestic fuel, plastic wood, snow tires, charcoal, insulation and packaging materials, wood flour and soil aids. Like wood chips, it is a significant source of supply for the pulp mills.

Provincial foresters are now applying genetics to give nature an assist and produce larger trees faster. Experiments in air-borne fertilization are being undertaken. Entomologists are striving to control insect enemies. But it is with the seed program that results seem definite. The Forest Service in co-operation with industry, locates "plus" trees in the best stands and takes off scions for grafting to superior root stock in a plantation. The tree that results produces seeds of superior quality and in turn, superior trees.

Before 1958 Barkerville was a meagre collection of forlorn buildings peopled by a few old stalwarts. By 1868 it was the largest city west of Chicago, north of San Francisco. It was named after Billy Barker, a Cornish seaman who jumped ship at Victoria to join the chase for Cariboo gold along with thousands of others. On a sultry day in August, 1862, down the creek from the majority of diggers, he found pay dirt 42 feet down. It proved to be a 600-foot strip that netted him a $600,000 fortune.

Four years previously, news of gold along the Fraser and Thompson rivers had spread as far as San Francisco. Suddenly, the rugged territory known only by Indians and Hudson's Bay Co. servants, was invaded by 30,000 men, mostly Americans. They flooded up the rivers and into the eastern creeks searching for the end-of-the-rainbow mother lode. They pushed on into the Cariboo and Barkerville where Barker's find created a deluge. From eastern Canada, the United States,

FIRE THE DESTROYER

Nature provides and nature destroys. In ten years between 1956 and 1965, lightning caused more forest fires than any other cause. In that time there were 21,059 fires and lightning started 7,766 of them. Campers caused 2,224. The fires of ten years have burned over 4.75 million acres and destroyed standing timber estimated to be almost $33 million. It has cost the people of British Columbia an average of almost $1.9 million a year for those ten years, to fight and extinguish the fires. A bad year was 1961 when 1.25 million acres were razed. It is not exactly accurate to say: "only you can prevent forest fires" ... *but you can help!*

China and Europe men came with the gold fever burning hot in their eyes. And the girls came too. A dance with a "hurdy-gurdy" girl, as the men called them, was $10. Champagne bottles were used for 10-pins. The stern shadow of Matthew Baillie Begbie in his judge's black robe and white wig brought a measure of law and a semblance of order. Rough men grubbed in the muck, caroused and a few grew rich. Barker himself, in classic style, married a lady with expensive tastes and died penniless in a Victoria old people's home.

Gold is not so important now. Of 1965's mineral production, gold accounted for only about $4.4 million of an approximate $280 million mining total. The industry is producing gold, copper, silver, lead, zinc, molybdenum, iron and eight other metals, asbestos and seven other industrial minerals and six structural minerals, plus coal, oil and natural gas. As British Columbia's second industry, mining employs about 12,000 people with an annual payroll around $70 million. It accounts for five percent of the labour force.

Unlike forestry where the assets literally stand up to be counted, mining is a precarious business and only for the strong of heart. Despite the electro-mechanical aids to mineral exploration the risk of finding ore in economic amounts is such that no taxes are levied for the first three years after production begins. After that, 10 percent is collected on the net profit.

Copper and molybdenum are the two minerals getting most of the attention in the mid-sixties. Copper, with its present production value of about $35 million, expected to reach $70 million by 1970, has nine operating mines with some 20 under development or active construction. Production of molybdenum has only just begun but is expected to be valued at $45 million by 1970. Three mines are producing now and some 15 are under development or active construction. It is called the space age metal because it is vital to steel alloys. Known deposits of other minerals like tungsten, mercury and manganese await production as requirement demands. In the mid-sixties the province has 26 important metal mines of all types in operation, with another 50-odd under construction or active development.

Japan has been the spark plug and major market for British Columbia's mineral production. In 1965, Japan imported 205 million tons of raw materials from world sources. It cost the Japanese $3.2 billion. As part of that program, the country has guaranteed itself 122,000 tons of copper a year by signing long-term contracts for the outputs of mines in Canada, the Philippines, Bolivia, Australia and the Transvaal. Japan has to import 96 percent of its iron ore to keep its steel mills hot and its supershipyards fed. Part of that amount comes from six iron mines along the British Columbia coast where the Japanese have spent millions helping to finance the mines, docks and townsites as well as the special ore carriers designed for the Pacific transport. Japan is the province's only iron ore customer. Coking coal is the other commodity needed by Japan's steel industry, the world's third largest. Ninety percent of British Columbia's coal goes to Japan from the fields of Crowsnest Industries Ltd. at Michel-Natal near the Alberta border, where there are proven reserves of 50 million tons. Already importing almost a half million tons of Crowsnest coal a year, Japan is seeking a guarantee of at least two million tons a year. A sidelight to the Japanese entry into provincial mining activity are the 20 offices of large Japanese trading and industrial houses in Vancouver.

Ore concentration facilities have a present capacity of 64,000 tons a day. More concentrators are being built and by 1970 it is expected the potential will be 130,000 tons a day. Exploration is continuing at an unprecedented pace. An estimated total of $35 million was spent for exploration in 1965-1966, the amount spent for the entire 10 years between 1951 and 1961.

Mining has come a long way from the Barkerville days. No longer is it a pick-and-shovel business. The industry has changed from one of high grade, low tonnage to one of low grade, high tonnage. The advent of magnificent mining machinery, better blasting and processing techniques, the dedication of men educated to the profession and trained to their equipment and the amount of money available from the sale of public shares in the ventures has made of British Columbia mining in the mid-sixties a bold, busy, surging industry. Only one cloud shadows the scene — a shortage of skilled manpower, which is peculiar neither to the province nor to the mining industry elsewhere. A skilled man in the industry may earn $45 a day but it is a remote life. Although not the beans-and-bacon and tent-town life of a few years ago, it is still less attractive than a city job where well-paid construction projects exist in abundance.

Big tough men in small tough ships — after 50 years of power boat fishing, that in essence, is still the way of life along the British Columbia coast. Nevertheless time has brought its changes. There used to be 70-odd canneries from Victoria to Prince Rupert. Now there are 24 automated modern plants with big flash freezers. Local marine architects have developed boat designs better fitted to local conditions and the boats are more seaworthy. Most of them are equipped with fathometers for fish detection and navigation. Most have radio-telephones. All have the latest synthetic nets, ropes and other gear. The larger craft have fog-piercing radar. But with all the advances and increased catch efficiency the old story is much the same: rugged men in dauntless little ships in competition with a big, merciless ocean.

Fishing is British Columbia's oldest industry. It began in 1870, the year salmon-canning started on the lower Fraser River. Before that there had been a flourishing era of whaling, and of fur-sealing which ended with the Pelagic Sealing Treaty of 1911. A Vancouver trader found an economical way to fish for halibut in the 1880's. He towed Indians out to the fishing grounds and gathered their catches in his larger boat. Thirty years later, when the Grand Trunk Pacific Railway completed its line to Prince Rupert from the east, it made that centre the world's halibut capital. It still is.

Canadians are not fish eaters. When they are they choose only the choicest halibut and the reddest salmon steaks. Their per capita consumption is only 13 pounds a year. To satisfy the domestic market the small boat method of fishing is adequate. Meanwhile a Russian fleet works outside the 12-mile limit in 400-man floating factories, accompanied by catcher boats, salvage tug and fuelled by their tankers, shovelling in and processing many varieties of ground-fish Canadians have ignored. One sign that the industry means to encourage the consumption of ground-fish like gray and black cod, ocean perch and sole, is the new $4 million B.C. Packers Ltd. plant at Steveston at the mouth of the Fraser River. It is designed to freeze and market 30 million pounds of ground-fish fillets a year.

A sore point bothers coast fishermen. It is the fact that other whaling nations have not accepted the biological evidence that the annual whale kill must be reduced. Their floating factories, if they continue unabated, will soon make it certain the north Pacific and Arctic mammals will become extinct. Once a great industry, whaling is represented now on the British Columbia coast by only one station in an old RCAF wartime patrol base at Coal Harbour, northern Vancouver Island. There, B.C. Packers, partnered by a Japanese company, process about 800 whales a season. The grading is done by a precision team of temporarily-imported Japanese nationals. Most of the dark red, protein-rich meat, flash-frozen in 40-pound chunks, ends up combined with tuna, cereals and spices, as Tokyo ballpark *hotto doggu's*. Some goes to California for pet food. Every ounce of tons of bone and waste is reduced to many grades of oil and meal used in at least 500 products from lipsticks to paint to plastics to space-age lubricants. But not a pound of succulent, protein-rich whale meat is consumed at Canadian tables.

The British Columbia coast fishing fleet comprises some 7,300 boats. Seventy percent of the fish are taken by 30 percent of the fishermen, of which there are about 10,000. There are some 4,000 tendermen and shore workers. In 1965, although fish products were valued at $84.6 million, 40 percent of the boats earned less than $1,000. Only five percent of the boats normally earn between $10,000 and $30,000.

Salmon is the most important species and is fished largely in waters off the Fraser, Skeena and Nass rivers, Smith Inlet and Rivers Inlet and the waters off the Queen Charlotte Islands and Vancouver Island. The size of the seasonal catch depends on many chance factors. For example, prolonged dry spells shrink rain-fed streams and the salmon cannot enter them to spawn. Autumn rainstorms create floods that scour the gravel bottoms of streams and destroy the salmon spawn. The return of the salmon to their birthplace is an ages-old miracle that touches all British Columbians. Every autumn thousands of people stand on the banks of streams to watch silently as nature replays its life-and-death story.

That there are too many salmon fishermen and too many boats is indicated by this fact: the value of the year's salmon catch has more than doubled in 20 years but the actual total catch weight has remained relatively unchanged.

Fish were the first of British Columbia's natural resources to be used by man. Long before white men arrived the Indian had become expert in the use of the salmon spear. Smoked salmon was his staple food along the coast. Today many Indians fish commercially; most own their own boats, many, large seiners – thus achieving a greater opportunity for independence than provided by any other occupation. Even that situation may be changing, as each year a growing number of Indians graduate from vocational schools to take their places in industry.

What keeps a man wrestling the sea? The independent life and the chance of a bonanza catch. Each year some lose both.

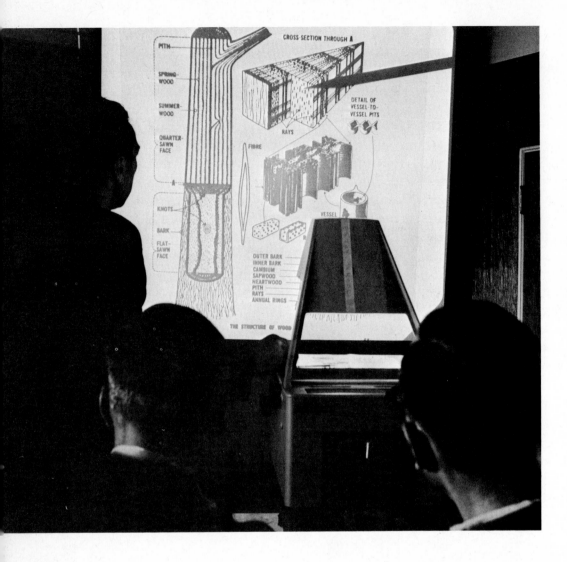

CROSS-SECTION THROUGH A

PITH

SPRING-
WOOD

SUMMER-
WOOD

QUARTER-
SAWN
FACE

A

KNOTS

BARK

FLAT-
SAWN
FACE

DETAIL OF
VESSEL-TO-
VESSEL PITS

RAYS

FIBRE

VESSEL

OUTER BARK
INNER BARK
CAMBIUM
SAPWOOD
HEARTWOOD
PITH
RAYS
ANNUAL RINGS

THE STRUCTURE OF WOOD

THE FOREST SERVICE training school has graduated 375 forest rangers and assistant rangers since it began in 1949. Course includes forest management, protection, fire suppression, forest mensuration, surveying and silviculture study.

300-YEAR-OLD HEMLOCK, containing 5,000 board feet of lumber, twisting as it falls, crashes to the moss floor of the forest at Juskatla in the Queen Charlotte Islands. The faller is George Merchison who is also pictured on page four.

Men and the Tools to Reap the Harvest

There are thirteen photographs in this section. They span the length and breadth and ceiling and cellar of British Columbia. From the Queen Charlottes, opposite, to the coal of Michel (page 55) near the Alberta border, it is 817 air miles. From Cassiar's asbestos, near the top of the province (page 54) it is 738 air miles to the Craigmont open pit at Merritt (page 53) in the south of the province. The Cassiar tramline photograph was taken in a high chilling wind almost a mile above sea level. The head-lamped diamond driller at Kimberley was portrayed a half mile below the surface in the silent, dark damp. The harvest of abundance is far-reaching.

HEAVY-POWERED STEEL BOOM BOATS are the cutting horses of a watery corral as they flit like water bugs among the logs, sorting them for size, species and quality. Sometimes they are called 'dozer boats. Here at Juskatla many of the drivers are Haida Indians.

A COAST TROLLER FISHERMAN waits in his cabin doorway at a fishing company dock to be unloaded of his day's salmon catch. Many trollermen fish alone. They usually have four lines out at the same time, two off the stern and one line each from long outrigger poles.

A MORNING'S CATCH OF YOUNG SALMON is unloaded from a seiner's hold at the modern processing plant at Namu on Fitz Hugh Sound, a few miles from the open Pacific. The industry provides steady employment for hundreds of Indians, many of whom own their boats.

A SALMON SEINER lies close to its big net in Fitz Hugh Sound as it tightens the ring to gather the silver horde of salmon. A seiner usually has a crew of seven.

THE TROLLER *B.C. Lady* moves out of the harbour at Prince Rupert to fish in Chatham Sound off the mouth of the Skeena. Frozen catch may end up in Le Havre.

FLEET SUPPLY SHIP, *Tyee Shell* (left), covers 60,000 miles yearly to service boats and camps with petroleum fuels. One of five, ship carries 530,000 gallons.

OPEN PIT OF CRAIGMONT MINES LTD. near Merritt in the Nicola Valley, 700 feet deep, represents 40 million tons of excavation in five years of which a quarter was copper ore (1.8 percent). Underground workings begin soon. Concentrator produces 5,000 tons a day of chalcopyrite. It is all shipped to Japan's smelters.

TRAMLINE OF CASSIAR ASBESTOS CORPORATION moved most of 1965's 743,700 tons of ore from 6,000-ft. level to concentrator below. 1965 sales were $17.5 million.

COKING COAL OF CROWSNEST PASS COAL CO. at Michel is water-washed, then drum-dried by heat of this flame. Japan buys total output.

ROD MILL CONCENTRATOR of Brynnor Mines Ltd., Torquart Bay, on Vancouver Island's west coast, produces powdered iron ore for Japan, shipped from own dock.

DEEP UNDERGROUND IN THE SULLIVAN MINE of Cominco Ltd., Kimberley, a 25-year hard-rock diamond driller, Bud Krown, prepares a series of holes for blasting.

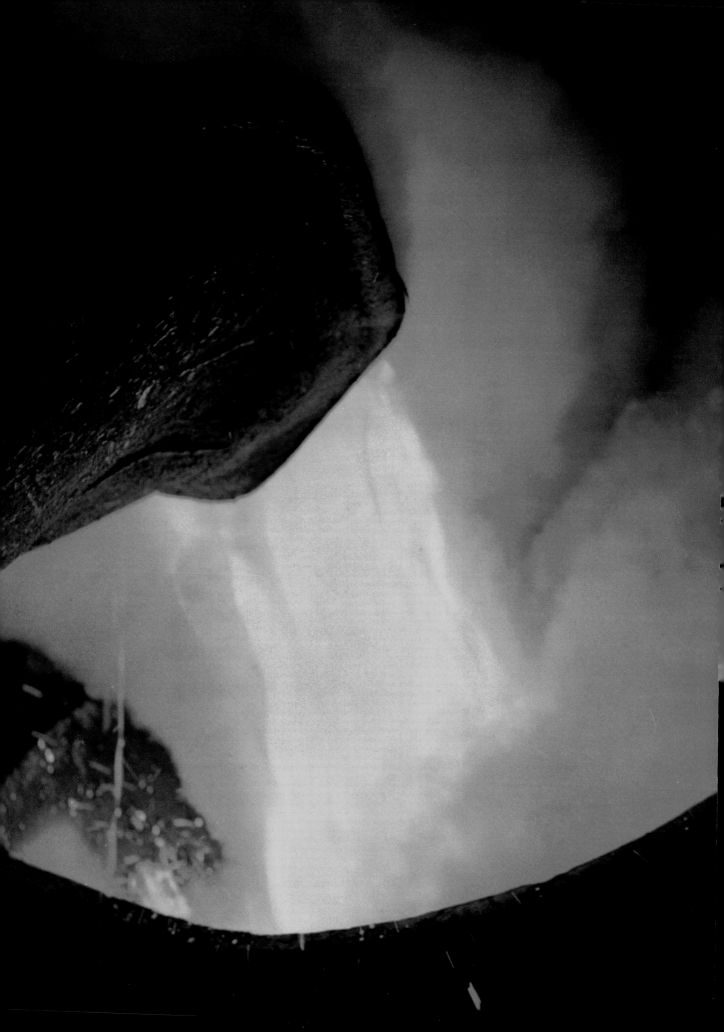

5

A Varied Economy

A popular description of Canada is a ribbon of people and industry that borders the United States. The hard fact is that British Columbia has turned the ribbon northward 700 miles and has dotted it with hustle and bustle as it unwound. The impetus was provided by the wartime construction of the Alaska Highway which made the great Peace River, Fort St. John and Fort Nelson areas accessible. All but 300 miles of the 1,523-mile-long highway between Dawson Creek in the Peace and Fairbanks, Alaska, lie within Canada. Soon after its completion the discovery of great oil and natural gas deposits was made and, with a spreading forest products industry and new

mineral finds along the route up from the coast, a new industrial belt was promised. With the construction of the John Hart Highway joining the Peace with Prince George, and the Pacific Great Eastern Railway linking the north with Vancouver, the promise is being fulfilled. Crossroads have become towns; some towns, small thriving cities. Petroleum is mainly responsible.

The subterranean basement underlying the Peace country is a geological continuation of the Alberta oil fields. It is proving to be a similar treasure vault. Between 1957 and 1966 the average of gas reserves per well drilled was 4.6 billion cubic feet. The United States average for the same period was 1.4 billion cubic feet and for

Alberta it was 1.77 billion cubic feet. The proven reserves of gas are estimated to be a colossal seven trillion cubic feet with a potential of over 90 trillion cubic feet. The proven reserves of oil and liquid hydrocarbons are estimated at 500 million barrels. What their potential is has yet to be fully determined.

Between 1951 and 1964, the major oil companies spent $600 million for exploration in the province. It cost them another $355 million for production costs and government royalties. In 1965, provincial gas wells produced 171.5 billion cubic feet of natural gas, while the 495 oil wells of the province poured out 13.5 billion barrels of oil. There were many by-products, principally butane, propane and sulphur.

The province owns its gas and oil lands in entirety and thus the resource provides a substantial amount of provincial revenue. Unlike the forest products industry, which reclaims some of its taxes in fire control and other services, provincial revenue from petroleum is almost expense free. Executives within the industry say it has one of the highest rates of per capita return to government of any resource industry within the province.

The Canadian industrial ribbon enters British Columbia in its southeast corner – the 19-million-acre region of the East and West Kootenays where 110,000 people live and work. It is a blue and green sportland of lakes and forests lying among the Rocky, Monashee, Selkirk and Purcell mountains. A large number of people who live there work for Cominco Ltd., formerly Consolidated Mining & Smelting Co. of Canada Ltd. Many others work for companies supplying goods or services to Cominco whose heart is Trail, the largest city of the Kootenays. It is the site of the world's largest smelters of silver, lead, zinc and other minerals.

It is estimated that since 1906 the company has generated more than $3 billion worth of primary wealth in the region. Since World War II, the company has paid a half billion dollars in wages alone. It employs 6,000 people. Since 1945 it has spent $150 million on expansion and modernization. In any year of the sixties it will buy $20 million worth of supplies from 1,000 provincially-based suppliers. In 1965 its production within the province was valued at $200 million. That year its tax bill was over $11 million.

Cominco produced 432,000 tons of lead and zinc in 1965, seven percent of the world's supply. Most of the ore came from its gigantic Sullivan mine at Kimberley. From Sullivan also came six million ounces of silver. The Kootenay chemical plants produced 600,000 tons of fertilizer and thousands of tons of acids and industrial chemicals. The whole complex requires six hydroelectric plants, loading docks at tidewater, affiliated mines elsewhere in the nation and sales offices and subsidiary plants in Canada and other parts of the world. The 2,000-man engineering group is forever active, plotting new markets.

Until recent years the Kootenays were tucked away in a corner, with closer ties to Alberta communities just across the boundary than to the Lower Mainland. Now No. 3 Highway is complete from the Alberta border to Hope, hugging the 49th parallel all the way. This route has had the effect of establishing closer economic and social ties between the Kootenays and the southwest part of the province.

Northwest, 300 miles from the peaks and valleys of the Kootenays, is the storied Cariboo, an elevated, rolling plateau. The surrounding timbered slopes and snow-clad crags yield suddenly to gentle grassland and willows but no mountains can be seen from its centre. This is the land of a vanishing breed of tall, easy, reticent men in dusty saddles and worn denims who are fence menders, branders, horsebreakers, hay pitchers, irrigators, welders and machinery tenders all in one. It is a country of big ranches like the immense Gang Ranch and further to the south in the Nicola country, the ranch of the Douglas Lake Cattle Company, as big as the province of Prince Edward Island. Against the backdrop of the moving mural of white-faced Herefords, the sounds heard are of steers bawling, the wind whining, the crying of loons in the reeds of the little jewel-like lakes.

The Cariboo country was first populated by American gold-seekers. Now the Americans are returning but this time they seek land. Some 50 percent of the ranches that changed ownership in the past decade were bought by investors from the United States who, harassed in their home states by high costs and population pressures, are seeking a happier life. The immigrants have brought new capital and the know-how needed for modern ranch operation.

Though Canadians and Americans eat little fish, they more than make up for the lost protein by eating beef. Their normal consumption is 80 pounds a year. In 1965, the British Columbia Department of Agriculture reported 43,000 head of beef, the biggest percentage from the Cariboo, were sold in the United States. This was a great increase over previous years.

Recent years have brought development of feeder lots where range-bred cattle are stuffed with grain and "finished" before killing. Although the province raises enough beef for its own requirement, and some feeder lots are now operating in the Fraser Valley, a large number of provincial cattle go to Alberta for finishing before being returned to British Columbia meat packers. The result is that almost 61 percent of the beef slaughtered in Vancouver is labelled "government choice."

The Thompson plateau forms the southern part of the Cariboo. Between it and the Monashee Mountains in the east, lies the Okanagan Valley. Narrow, not 100 miles long, housing the cities of Vernon, Kelowna and Penticton, the valley was a dehydrated Eden that stirred itself when water was added.

In the 1870's when an Oblate Mission priest planted the first apple seedlings there was neither power nor pump to lift the water from the valley-centred Lake Okanagan even the few feet to the surrounding benchland. Instead, using gravity, water was brought down from the hilltop lakes in long, gradually-descending wood flumes. The higher lakes are still the source but the water is now piped under pressure to the valley ranches and vineyards. Many have sprinkler systems. Today the lake's shores are verdant and productive, another example of man's power to make the desert bloom. Just beyond the irrigated edges, the dry range country crackles with long-thorned cactus and the rattlesnakes' warning may be heard in the hot sun.

By provincial law, fruit producers of

the Okanagan must market their crops through a grower-owned co-operative society. Called B.C. Tree Fruits Ltd., the operation includes three large juice and processing plants. In the 25 years beginning in 1940, the co-operative has handled 125 million bushel boxes of apples with a return to the growers of some $375 million. It is estimated that among the 3,450 orchards consisting of 35,600 planted acres, there are some 2.3 million fruit trees. Slightly more than half the tree-farm acreage produces 10 kinds of apples. The rest is devoted to pears, plums, peaches, apricots, cherries and grapes. The co-op has $23 million invested in packing houses and cold storage plants, the latter with a capacity of 7.25 million bushel boxes of apples. The co-op ships to 30 countries.

The Okanagan also produces, in order of value, dairy products, beef, poultry, vegetables and grain. It is not generally known that the district sells more beef a year ($3 million) than the Fraser Valley ($2.3 million). The Cariboo is first in this respect, the Kamloops area is second and the Okanagan is third.

From the 49th parallel to the 54th parallel, British Columbia's eastern boundary follows roughly the crest line of the Rocky Mountains. At the 54th parallel the boundary follows the 120th meridian as far as the 60th parallel which is the border of the Northwest Territories. The approximate 20,000 square miles of foothills and plain lying between the Rockies and the Alberta boundary belong geographically to Alberta. Another distinct empire was added to British Columbia's roster of geo-economic areas when an Imperial Act of Parliament awarded it to the coast province. This is the Peace River country where Alexander Mackenzie established one of the first trading posts in the northwest in 1793.

The construction of the Alaska Highway gave wartime impetus to the area. The activity increased when gas was discovered. An example is Fort St. John. In 1945, its population was 700. In the mid-sixties, it was 7,000. Some 40,000 people live in the Peace River district now and each one of them is a tough individualist with a temperament attuned to the environment. He endures dust, heat and bugs through the hot summer. He survives the dry, piercing cold in the bleak winters. Between seasons he battles mud. He is an impatient frontiersman who grows grain by the square mile, produces natural gas to feed the fires of a great section of the western side of the continent, brings petroleum bubbling up thousands of drill holes, cuts timber and pulpwood in significant amounts, breeds excellent livestock and develops some of the nation's finest grain seed. Fort St. John is Canada's largest seed-shipping centre.

To a greater degree perhaps than any other rural area, the Peace offers a variety of opportunity in many fields of endeavour to young men with training, ambition and muscle who are stirred to test their resolution in a search for a rewarding and highly satisfying way of life for themselves and for their families.

Only two percent of the province is suitable for farming. Notwithstanding, the provincial total of farm cash receipts from the sale of all farm products in 1965 was $154 million. The province has many farming areas. Excluding the Cariboo and the Okanagan, the two largest are the Peace River country and the delta of the Fraser River known as the Fraser Valley. The latter produces about half the total value of provincial agricultural products. In particular, it is the breadbasket for the half of the province's population that lives in metropolitan Vancouver and Vancouver Island. The Fraser Valley accounts for 97 percent of the egg and dairy requirements, all of the poultry, some of the fruit, half of the vegetables. There are 2,300 dairy farmers on the Lower Mainland who reap some $22 million a year from milk. It is 70 percent of their income.

Cause for concern is the urban sprawl pushing out like lava from the congestion of Vancouver and New Westminster. It now occupies 100 of the 800 square miles on the black-loamed valley floor. Every time the metropolitan area adds another 1,000 people, 380 acres of valley farmland vanish. The monumental problem facing the municipal and provincial governments is the space shortage for a fast-growing population which is surrounded by water or mountains on three sides. If the trend continues there will be only 160,000 acres of farmland left in the valley by 1980. That is 40,000 acres short of the acres needed to maintain the *present* proportion of food-producing acres to population.

There are many proposals. One by the Lower Mainland Regional Planning Board suggests an enforceable land use scheme whereby the upland areas would be developed on each side of the valley for housing and communities. This would leave the still useable farmland below to raise vital food supplies . . . The ice age uncovered abundance as it retreated but it left a shortage of living space.

All that has been described so far has been of an abundance of resources, in quality and quantity in excess of those owned by many countries of the world. British Columbia has something else. It is a resource that is not cut down, dug up or taken away and it is not just mere scenery. Rather it is the Great Outdoors with all the expression implies. It is an escapist's Utopia. Much of the province seems an endless wilderness but a lot of it can be viewed from a comfortable car on a modern highway, with a good dinner and a swim in a motel pool at the end of the day's drive. With more and more people devoting their leisure to touring and outdoor recreation, the province has become such an attraction that almost three times as many people visit it in the tourist season as live in it.

In 1965, there were 5.1 million tourist visitors. They spent $201.1 million – $10 million more than in 1964. It is expected that figures of future years will far surpass those of the mid-sixties.

In contrast with the development of other resources, the costs of tourism to the government are relatively few in comparison to the revenue. Some say that everything beyond the few hundred thousand dollars spent on advertising and Travel Bureau services is a gain. Others wonder if the $200 million income isn't cancelled by a roughly comparable amount British Columbians spend holidaying in Hawaii, Mexico, the United States and elsewhere. This group criticizes those who exclaim over the Swiss Alps and have never seen Mount Robson, or parents whose children have visited Disneyland three times but Barkerville never.

The highways, vantage points, hotels, motels and government campsites are packed with out-of-province tourists from May to September. The completion of the Rogers Pass section of the Trans-Canada Highway opened a new doorway from the east and changed the pattern of entry into the province. It has replaced the old southern border route through Blaine, Washington, as the main entrance. Now, 39 percent of visitors are Canadian and they account for almost half the tourist spending. Calgarians are 12 percent of the total tourists. Visitors from Seattle, Edmonton, Los Angeles, San Francisco, Portland, Regina, Saskatoon, Winnipeg and Toronto follow in that order. Canadians want the outdoor attractions while most Americans stay in the cities. The Lower Mainland enjoys the big share of the total tourist income. Of 1965's revenue, $160 million was spent there. The Vancouver Visitors Bureau serviced half a million inquiries that year, 40 percent more than in 1964.

Scenery is the main interest of 55 percent of the visitors. The survey shows further that 17 percent list "friendliness of the people" as the prime reason for their visit. Outdoor activities draw 10 percent; gardens, 7 percent; parks, 4 percent. An additional dividend appears in the number of tourists who consider moving to the province following an initial visit. One official source states that an average of 100 settlement inquiries a month are received and many of these have resulted in permanent residence.

The recognition of abundance is not new in British Columbia. It is as old as the coastal Indians whose civilizations were developed on a plentiful supply of necessities which, seemingly inexhaustible, could be won without too much work. As Ruth Benedict, anthropologist, points out in her book, *Patterns of Culture*, affluence was the mark of strength and greatness in the world of the west coast Indian. The extent of a chief's wealth in the form of blankets made from down, carved canoes and heavy copper plaques was the measure of both his dignity and his might. Confrontations were sometimes resolved by destroying quantities of such wealth in sight of the opponents — one aspect of a potlatch. The side which destroyed the most was the moral victor.

It was destruction of great primitive art, only fully appreciated now, for the Indians made even utilitarian tools beautiful. Their totem poles, still carved frequently, have given the province a symbol of identification known around the world.

Today, British Columbia has 42,000 Indians in 192 bands, the population having increased 46.7 percent since 1950. Over 35,000 live on the 1,618 reserves supervised by a federal government agency. More and more, Indians are entering the mainstream of provincial life with the greatest opportunities provided by the forest and fishing industries. More than 12,000 attended school in 1965, half of them in non-Indian schools. They are enfranchised and one of them is a Member of the Legislative Assembly.

There are 10 language divisions among the many Indian groups and there is little communion between them. Among them are the Haida of the Queen Charlottes, the Tsimshian of the north, the Kwakiutl of the coast fiords, the Nootka of western Vancouver Island, the Bella Coola of the central coast, the Déné of the northern interior, the Coast Salish and the Interior Salish, and the Kootenay who live in the southeastern corner of the province.

RED SPARTAN APPLES, cross between Newtown and McIntosh Red, are checked by orchardist Brian Porter, Kelowna

The Elements Combined

Photographs are images of tangible things and books have only a specific number of pages. To make the aerial photograph of Mount Robson (page 65) symbolize the thousand-faceted scenery of British Columbia is to say a grain of sand is the desert. It is equally difficult to make Chief Dan George represent the 192 Indian bands, or the Spartan apples (above) stand for the cornucopia of the fruit industry. In each of these themes as in all aspects of this photographers' provincial paradise, there are thousands of pictures. Single photos can only convey an idea. Imagine the rest.

PEACEFUL PEACE RIVER FARMLAND, lustrous in the early morning summer sunshine, awakens to a new day of lusty growth for which that fertile land is so famous.

CATTLE RANCHING IN B.C. (right) is exemplified by this corral scene at the Douglas Lake Ranch where foreman Mike Ferguson is cutting steers for shipment.

MAJESTIC MOUNT ROBSON, 12,972 feet, is the highest peak in the Canadian Rockies. Just inside the B.C. border, it is an attraction for thousands of tourists.

CHIEF DAN GEORGE of the Burrard band, North Vancouver, at 67 is a respected member of the B.C. community, a TV personality starring in a CBC series.

COMPRESSOR STATION at McLeod Lake, 90 miles north of Prince George on Hart Highway, is third of 13 such $5 million stations used to force natural gas south- ward to Vancouver from the Peace River country through the 30-inch underground pipeline. Crew of 12 maintains the four diesels developing 14,200 h.p.

DAIRY FARMING and mixed agriculture industry thrive between the mountains in the lower mainland's Fraser Valley. Growing city of Chilliwack is seen in distance.

TWENTY-FIVE MILLION 2-YEAR-OLD SEEDLINGS yearly are taken from Forest Service seed beds such as these and transplanted in the logged areas throughout B.C.

ONLY THE SCENERY DIFFERS (right). This view of drilling exploration at a potential ore site is almost a permanent facet of the rich British Columbia landscape.

HOLLY FOR CHRISTMAS, shipped across Canada, is gathered from this 54-year-old tree in Victoria. This 2-acre farm of 450 trees yields about eight tons a year.

6

The Surge of the Sea

"Who hath desired the sea? – the sight of salt water unbounded. The heave and the halt and the hurl and the crash of the comber wind-hounded." The year Kipling wrote those lines the first cargo of wheat left the port of Vancouver. Much has happened in the 70-odd years since 1895 to dispel some but not all of the 19th century mystery of the sea. Something subtle still seems to happen to people who live beside it. They are relaxed and they are romantic. Peter Freuchen wrote in his *Book of the Seven Seas:* "The sight of foreign seamen or of tall ships from far away or even of an exotic bit of merchandise from halfway around the world or even of an oddly shaped scrap of driftwood cast up on the beach gives any of us a pang of jealousy of the men who move about over the sea viewing the wonders of the deep."

And what wonders there are for the ship watchers now. On almost any day Vancouverites may read in their morning paper, items like: "Imagine a ship with six holds, two of which are each able to carry more cargo than a wartime Liberty ship normally loading 10,000 tons. Imagine a ship with solid hatch covers weighing 41 tons each, lifted by an enormous travelling crane riding on rails on deck. Such a ship is the Greek *M.S. Pentas,* now in port on her maiden voyage to load 32,000 tons of grain for Europe, an outstanding example of the huge bulk carriers now travelling the ocean highways." And they are getting bigger. One Vancouver wharf complex is preparing for 1970 when it will dock and bulk-load its first 100,000 tonner. But in the mid-sixties the coastal ship watchers have plenty to see.

In 1965 the 74 pilots of the Pilotage Authority had some 9,000 assignments. They averaged about 40 a day, not including coastal shipping and vessels under 200 tons. It meant that 4,307 deep-sea ships took on cargoes or discharged cargoes at the 29 ports of the British Columbia coast where the accommodation ranges from the single berth at Torquart on Vancouver Island's west coast to the 79 berths at the Port of Vancouver. Of the 1965 total, Vancouver was host to 1,878 vessels and the nearby Port of New Westminster on the Fraser River, with its special advantage of fresh water that cleans barnacled hulls, added to the activity. Each year brings a slight reduction in the number of visiting deep-sea ships but the total tonnage of cargo increases. Illustrating the new look in international shipping is the super-freighter, 600 feet long and more, with a high degree of automation and instrumentation.

In 1965, exports to foreign countries from all the British Columbia ports were 15,615,500 tons. Imports through these ports were 2,716,000 tons. The export of seaborne lumber was 2,439,444,559 board feet, an increase of 156.7 million board feet over 1964. The increase was equal to the cargoes of 30 ships. Despite a grain handlers' strike, 196,137,500 bushels poured out of the elevators into the yawning holds.

Vancouver is British Columbia's largest port. In 1965 it handled more than 20 million tons of dry cargo. This made it the busiest dry cargo port on the entire Pacific seaboard. Almost half that tonnage was exported to foreign markets. Lumber and logs shipped to other countries totalled 1.3 billion board feet; potash, 684,000 tons; fertilizer, 117,000 tons; sulphur, 747,000 tons. Nearly half a million tons of coal went to Japan from a new bulk-loading facility at Port Moody, up-harbour from Vancouver.

There is a true international flavour to the Port of Vancouver. Of the 1965 ship arrivals, 298 flew the Norwegian flag; 233, Japanese; 221, Greek; 200, Liberian; 199, United Kingdom; 144, United States; 109, German; followed in order by the flags of Sweden, China, Denmark, Netherlands, France, Italy and the Philippines. Twenty-three bore the hammer and sickle flag of the U.S.S.R. There were 106 other vessels from still other countries. Outbound, 677 headed west for the Orient, 494 steered south for Panama enroute to the United Kingdom and Europe, 170 were routed to Central and South America, 121 went to Australasia and there were 104 destined for the eastern United States seaboard.

The unprecedented sales of Canadian wheat and other grain to Russia and China have at times strained the Vancouver port facilities. The National Harbours Board however is now underway with a program of addition and modernization. It forecasts that before 1970 more potash for fertilizer than wheat, all of it from the great new Saskatchewan deposits, will be moving out of the port. One major dock complex, Vancouver Wharves Ltd., is in the process of preparing for that time and serves as a good example of the acceleration the port is experiencing in the sixties. The company began operation with one

C.C.G.S. TO THE RESCUE

Welcome sight to mariners in trouble are the trim red and white hulls of the Canadian Coast Guard Service. This is the 95-foot *C.C.G.S. Racer* of 2400 h.p. On the way to a rescue mission her twin screws drive her at 18 knots. With her sister ship *Ready* she ranges the coast from Victoria to Prince Rupert. Each operates with a crew of 18, with 12 on board at any one time. Besides the two cutters, there are four high-speed crash boats on coastal service. Under Capt. J. C. Barbour, Pacific Coast Guard Rescue Officer, the little fleet and its personnel of 63 were involved in 346 incidents in 1965. Of these about 200 were in the Vancouver-Victoria area.

berth in 1960. In 1966 it docked its 1,000th ship and handled its five millionth ton of cargo. Already the company had spent $9 million on four berths and had built two potash storage silos each costing $1 million. By 1970 the firm will have four more silos, each with a capacity of 47,000 tons. Its total investment will then be in the vicinity of $17 million.

Providing another vital coastal service are the towboats and the towboat men. The world's largest fleet of towboats works the British Columbia coast and in almost every harbour. Implacable as icebergs, staunch as the rocks they skirt, they are the real work horses of the coastal economy. Each year they get bigger. Most are locally designed and built. The largest is the *Gibraltar Straits* of Straits Towing Ltd., a 3,840-h.p., 140-foot titan. Among the supertugs only one is still a steamer. She is the famous 2,750-h.p. *Sudbury* of Island Tug & Barge Ltd., renowned for her gallant, far-ranging salvages into the teeth of mid-Pacific gales. Then there are

the barges. The floating freight platforms, flat, roofed or boxed, are of many sizes. They transport everything from wood chips, general freight and highway trailers to heavy machinery, prefabricated houses and railroad box cars. In 1966, MacMillan Bloedel Ltd. launched the world's two largest covered barges for the transportation of newsprint to California from the company's paper mills at Port Alberni and Powell River. Each is 356 feet long with 82-foot beam. On tow, behind a specially-designed and built towboat, each is two weeks on the voyage.

These craft are the working classes. The other side of the maritime social register is represented by the sleek white ladies of the P&O Line's *Oriana, Orsova,* the 45,000-ton giantess, *Canberra,* and others. The 20-odd yearly visits of the round-the-world cruise ships bring momentary glamour to the workaday life of Vancouver harbour when hundreds of passengers disembark and hundreds more embark. Vancouver accounts for 30 percent of P&O's North American business. On arrival days ship watchers throng the Stanley Park shore and fill the pier end. A band plays. The tour buses spread out through the city carrying passengers.

Unheralded and for the most part, un-noticed, is another group of sea-going visitors that tallied over a year might well be larger than the total P&O passengers. They travel on 12-passenger freighters so popular that reservations for accommodation must be made at least a year ahead. A half dozen such vessels leave Vancouver every week. Passenger amenities are in many cases more elegant than on some passenger liners and where this is the case, the fare is higher as well. Freighters of this class are not required to carry doctors so most shipping lines will not book passengers over age 65, some not over age 60. As a result a slightly younger age group usually travels the freighters.

As with all great seaports, a little wandering uncovers a variety of scenes and moods to be observed only in a seaport. The Port of Vancouver is no exception. There exists the busy life of the warehouse streets bordering the docks, the dismal, beery aura of skid row, the seamen's missions, always ready to help a mariner, and the ship chandleries full of bright brass binnacles, bronze fittings and the smell of rope. There is the sight of the slim gray hulls of naval ships slipping line astern through the Narrows, sometimes greeted by the red fireboat throwing purple water in gaudy welcome. There is the sound of a 21-gun salute as an American admiral's flagship comes for a visit and the return salute from a Canadian Artillery battery on Brockton Point in Stanley Park . . . Life by the sea is part of the allure of British Columbia.

PILOT OF B.C. PILOTAGE AUTHORITY climbs aboard 14,-300-ton Russian bulk carrier, *Otradnoe*, at Brotchie Ledge, three miles off Victoria. The vessel was on her maiden voyage to pick up 13,400 tons of grain.

Not So Pacific

If Magellan could see his Pacific Ocean now he wouldn't think it so tranquil. It has become laced and interlaced with the foaming wakes of the world's trading ships as they scurry busily across its tossing 70 million square miles. They carry the wealth of a nation to exchange it for the wealth of another. The ports bordering the great water are its doorways to the world of commerce. Out of the ports of British Columbia flow the treasures of western Canada while into and through them, enter other nations' products that Canada needs for progress. Here is the Port of Vancouver during the summer of 1966 when the mood was anything but pacific.

GREEK-OWNED *Treis Ierarchi*, 627 feet long and 24,000 tons dead weight, discharging her water ballast, threads First Narrows, arriving in Port of Vancouver to load 22,500 tons of wheat for a port in China.

ALBERTA WHEAT POOL elevators loaded 62.5 million bushels of grain into 211 ships, July 1965 to July 1966 crop year — equal to 32,000 boxcars. Elevators (right) are a third of port's capacity, move a third of grain.

ANY DAY IN 1966 the Port of Vancouver was a busy scene of world commerce. Soon it will be busier as the National Harbours Board commences construction of new facilities and modernization of old ones.

COMMISSIONED 1966, "*Captain Cook*" is typical of thousands of coastal towboats. Worth $350,000, she is 75 feet long, has a 21-foot beam and a 12-foot draft.

P&O LINES' *Oriana*, of 42,000 tons, with 2,000 passengers and 900 crew, ghosts through First Narrows, Vancouver, under Lion's Gate Bridge in a fall fog.

COMMISSIONED 1965, "*Greg Yorke*" is unique, million-dollar, self-propelled train ferry making two daily round trips between Vancouver Island and mainland.

7

To Link a Vastness

Thus far in this examination of British Columbia it has become evident that when the ice age died and the will was read the province inherited natural resources worth a king's ransom. But the trees on the mountain slopes do not become structural timber, siding, plywood or pulp and paper until they are cut and carried labouriously to mills. They do not produce their ultimate in government revenue, payrolls or dividends to stockholders until they reach a market, which may be half way around the world. Similarly, minerals are meaningless until they are removed and refined. Scenery languishes unappreciated until someone sees it. Tumbling white water is just so much foam and froth until its course is dammed, penstocks have led its charge through turbines and the power is hung up on hydroelectric lines to be conducted into factories and homes.

Before proceeding with mills, mines and power plants, certainly before the province could take its place as a major industrial economy, access had to be provided. At first progress was slow but in the post-war era, the provincial Department of Highways spent well over $1 billion for roads, tunnels, bridges and maintenance. In 1966 the Department's budget was almost $96 million. When the year began, British Columbia had 22,900 miles of open road and 3,700 miles of cleared or uncleared right-of-way that will be finished road shortly. Of the completed road mileage, 6,200 miles are paved. At one stage in the program, a few years ago, the total value of bridges being built exceeded the total value of all the bridges previously built in British Columbia since Confederation. There are now some 3,000 bridges of all types. End to end they would stretch 50 miles.

British Columbia's first major road is still its greatest. In 1861, Governor Douglas put the Royal Engineers to work to plan a 400-mile, 18-foot-wide wagon road from Yale to the Cariboo gold fields, and to discover a way through some of the most rugged sections of the Fraser canyon. The Cariboo road was a marvel of its time. Today, many millions of dollars later, a tunnelled section of it costing over $5 million a mile, its hairpin bends are gradual curves, the spindly bridges have been replaced with steel masterpieces, the skirting ledges have been tunnelled or walled and traffic thunders through the canyon at 60 mph. As with the Rogers Pass section of the Trans-Canada Highway, the real miracle is that there is a road at all.

So benign have engineers made that entire highway, truckers and tourists can reach Calgary from Vancouver in one long day. But it is still not benign in winter. Then the great blowers throw roostertails of snow. Royal Canadian Artillery howitzers, from pre-planned gun emplacements through the Rogers Pass, shell the heights to create small avalanches before they can become big ones. Weary road maintenance crews become heroes.

Their work is doubly appreciated by drivers of some 9,000 motor transports and 1500 buses who must provide major communications links between communities.

Geographically, British Columbia is no longer fully served by the nation's two giant railroads, Canadian Pacific Railway and Canadian National Railways. Their original design was to provide a national east-west route across a province that is now developing north-south.

The CPR was first with the steel which joined the new province with eastern Canada. As well, it made the nation a bridge between Europe and the Orient. The main line entered the province from Calgary, only one-fifth the way up the boundary, moved slightly southwest to Kamloops then buried itself in the Thompson and Fraser river canyons towards Vancouver.

Twenty-five years later, the Grand Trunk Pacific, clinging to the tradition, entered the province from Edmonton, a third the way up the eastern boundary, and pushed west to Prince Rupert. The Canadian Northern Railway came through the same pass and headed south for Kamloops. Then it accompanied the CPR down the same canyons into Vancouver, zigging from wall to wall as the CPR zagged. These two lines became the provincial portion of the amalgamation that is now the CNR system.

The CPR had also been forced by the competition offered by the U.S.-owned Great Northern Railway in the Kootenay and Boundary districts, to build the Crowsnest-Kettle Valley branch line, now abandoned in places. Excepting only the rail link from Terrace to service the new aluminum smelting city of Kitimat, neither transcontinental line has as yet extended its steel to new resources and to new areas under development.

Thus, all alone to serve the burgeoning northland and the booming central interior is the provincial government-owned Pacific Great Eastern Railway. Born 35 years too soon, now just past its half century, its real importance has only been evident in the post-war years.

The PGE is described sometimes as "not pacific, not great and not eastern," and eastern it isn't. At its beginning the largest block of construction capital was provided by the Great Eastern Railroad of England and the directors added "Pacific" to identify the new western enterprise. The resulting initials "PGE" have led to all sorts of rude nicknames. Like the Grand Trunk Pacific's "Get There Perhaps" and the Toronto, Hamilton & Buffalo's "Tried Hard and Busted," the PGE used to be called the "Prince George Eventually" and the "Please Go Easy." Time has now refuted the implied slander.

Neither is it great in comparison with North America's continent-spanning railroads, but it is virile, hustling, modern. It was one of the continent's first lines to be completely dieselized and the first to control its traffic by microwave. Along the entire length of the 789-mile main line from the north terminals of Fort St. John and Dawson Creek in the Peace River country, to the North Vancouver yards, engineer talks to engineer or to any district office by radiotelephone, voice-relayed along the mountain tops by the lofty microwave towers.

And it certainly isn't pacific. The PGE has grossed $15 to $20 million revenue a year through most of the sixties and it is expected to double that by 1970. By then there will be the freight from seven new pulp mills on its route plus two mills at the end of a new 100-mile spur. Its rolling stock roster is already 1,900 cars of all types, among them, 250 new wood and chip cars and 100 pulp and paper cars. Motive power is provided by 60 diesel-electric locomotives. There are 1,600 employees. Breaking an old tie with North Vancouver across the harbour from Vancouver, long its southern headquarters, the main yards and new operational offices have now been moved to Prince George, the hub of activity in the interior where by 1968, on company-owned land, a half billion dollars in private capital will be invested in plant, office and warehouse facilities. All of it, it is expected, will provide freight traffic for a major lifeline in a growing economic colossus.

Meanwhile, on the coast, the blue-trimmed, spanking white "Queens" of the provincially-owned British Columbia Ferry Authority push their round, purposeful bows between the mainland and Vancouver Island, through the lovely Gulf Islands, up the Sunshine Coast to Powell River and from Kelsey Bay, north of Campbell River on Vancouver Island, overnight to Prince Rupert, where a connection is made with the Alaska State Ferry system. On the Prince Rupert run, begun in 1966, a new $5 million ferry-liner is used, with excellent stateroom accommodation and beautifully furnished public areas.

To the end of 1965, after five years of operation, more than 15 million passengers and five million vehicles had been transported on all routes. In 1965 alone, four million passengers and 1.1 million vehicles were carried. Each year sees the system's traffic increase about 10 percent.

The ferry fleet services 19 ports with 23 vessels. Two more are planned, one of which will be a sister ship to the *Queen*

THE TWO MAJOR RAILWAYS

Here at Siska in the Fraser river canyon, a few rail-hours north of Vancouver, the famous twin bridges of the Canadian National Railways and the Canadian Pacific Railway symbolize the service of Canada's two major railway systems to British Columbia. Without the Thompson and Fraser canyons the province would have but two east-west rail routes. It was along these canyons in the 1880's the C.P.R. laid its first rails en route to the coast. When the Canadian Northern line came later, the surveyors were forced to the opposite side of the canyons wherever the C.P.R. had changed sides. Thus this view: C.P.R. owns the lower bridge; C.N.R. the upper.

of Prince Rupert for the Prince Rupert run. The Authority's payroll is $5.5 million for 1,400 employees. In number of ships, gross tonnage and revenue, it is one of the world's largest ferry systems. The Star Line of Hong Kong carries more passengers; the Washington State Ferries carry more vehicles. In a little more than five years, the Ferry Authority has attained world-wide recognition for the successful operation of government-run ferries and its advice is now being sought by delegations from many countries. Among countries watching the British Columbia operation closely are Scotland, Scandinavia, Malta and Hawaii.

To help train engineers and crews for the growing service, the Ferry Authority has entered into a training program with the Department of Education that includes navigation, the basics for advancement of deck personnel to deck officers, catering, fitting and welding, painting, furniture repairing, rigging and life-raft servicing. The program will provide the qualified staff

needed for replacements and further expansion . . . In the meantime, passengers find that earlier methods of instruction have produced and maintain, clean on-time ships manned by a courteous deck staff and stewards, helpful green-blazered hostesses for the tourist season and reasonably priced, well-prepared, large-portioned meals — not the least of which is absolutely the best clam chowder on the whole of the coast.

Perhaps the next monument erected in British Columbia should be to the memory of either the Wright Brothers or of Sikorsky, inventor of the helicopter. Large and small aircraft and the adaptable chopper play an indispensable role in the development of a province that was made-to-order for the kind of vital communication they alone can provide.

The province has the world's largest number of helicopters per capita. In the spring and summer there are well over 100 machines in the air from first light to sunset. Helicopters have participated in the original exploration and development of almost every recent mineral or oil find in the province. They are used in the construction of power lines and microwave systems. They patrol oil and gas pipelines, erect ski tows and sedan lifts, transport timber cruisers into virgin forests, work as electronically sophisticated land survey instruments, help prevent and suppress forest fires, rush accident victims and patients needing special surgery out to medical aid.

One of the world's largest commercial helicopter companies, Okanagan Helicopters Ltd., is based at Vancouver. In 1965, its 68 machines logged 28,000 revenue hours and earned $4 million gross. It has handled assignments ranging from the Canadian Arctic to the North Sea and East Pakistan. Its mountain flying school has graduated pilots for the armed forces of the United States, the United Kingdom, France and Canada.

There are 1,143 fixed wing aircraft registered in the province . Of these, 696 are privately owned. The remaining 447 belong to 58 aircraft companies of which 41 are charter operators scattered all over the province, ready to put their Beavers, Cubs and Apaches into any off-beat corner a hunting party wishes, or to rush a big bulldozer part to a held-up crew. B.C. Airlines Ltd., largest of the small plane operators, is actually a scheduled airline. Its 34 Mallards, Beavers, Goose, Cessnas and Founds, are float-equipped or amphibian. The company made 70,000 revenue flights in 1965, carried 90,000 passengers, 77,600 ton-miles of freight and 11,800 ton-miles of mail. It serves over 400 places on the coast from Vancouver to Prince Rupert and from Vancouver Island to the Queen Charlottes. Its thunderbird-crested aircraft made over 300 emergency mercy flights in 1965. The orange emblazoned machines of the Royal Canadian Air Force also provide this vital service.

The fifth link in the chain of communications that makes the vast province a workable entity is the $450 million system of the British Columbia Telephone Co. Unlike Alberta where there are some 840 small phone companies, and Ontario where 160 of them exist apart from the Bell Telephone system, the province has only three small companies servicing about 40,000 phones other than B.C. Tel's 750,000 phone network. In addition some 3,800 boats have radiotelephone equipment. In 1966 the company was spending $1 million weekly on expansion facilities, 36 percent of it in its interior and northern divisions. Its microwave towers and relay stations stand tall on the mountaintops and lonely on sea-girt rocks, symbols of a new age.

The province is also well served in another communications field: press, radio and television. There are many consumer and industrial journals, locally edited and produced. There are more than 125 daily and weekly newspapers. The Vancouver daily papers are read all over the province. Eight television stations and 32 radio stations, together with many repeater stations for both media, are scattered in key localities to provide the greatest coverage. In some places they provide the only link with the world outside. These are the stations which program daily message periods for people who can communicate no other way. For such is the vastness.

KINNAIRD BRIDGE, graceful, distinctive, unique, is the province's newest span, now completed. It crosses the Columbia River a few miles south of Castlegar, not far from Arrow Dam.

SWEATING MEN in choking dust and summer heat, jockey an air drill into the granite south of Blue River on the route of the new Yellowhead Highway which will connect Kamloops with Jasper, Alberta.

With Men and Determination

For over a century, British Columbia has waged an expensive battle with its topography in an effort to bring unity to a land where isolation was inherent. Without pass-threading roads, rock-boring tunnels, canyon-cutting railways, inlet-delving coast boats, freighting airplanes, flitting helicopters, thrusting microwave towers, life would still be isolated. In some places it would be as remote as the life in Tibetan lamaseries on their scattered hilltops ... Even more important the abundant resources would still be largely unknown and undeveloped. To link this vastness has been both difficult and costly, but with persistence and determination, men, machines and money have progressively transformed byways into highways, made the crooked straight, and forged new and often startling life-lines.

NEW SALMO-CRESTON SECTION of the southern trans-provincial highway, 40 miles long, climbs to 5,800 feet altitude, the highest highway in the B.C. system.

NORTH COUNTRY WEATHER CONDITIONS are radio-relayed to Dept. of Transport "met" office by such remote trading post men as Wes Westfall, Germansen Landing.

FREE RIVER FERRIES like this one at Cedarvale crossing of the Skeena River are held by a suspended cable and are pushed sideways across river by the current.

HELICOPTERS are made-to-order work horses for the rough B.C. terrain. Pontoons nosed to the slope, an Okanagan Hiller disembarks a B.C. Hydro line crew.

MICROWAVE STRUCTURES (left) thrust into the skies of the province. This is B.C. Tel's Calvert Island substation, 60 miles north of the tip of Vancouver Island.

PACIFIC GREAT EASTERN RAILWAY engineer Donald Generous, 14 years service, at controls of 75-car downbound freight carrying pulp, grain, sulphur, lumber.

THE ULTRAMODERN FERRIES of the B.C. Ferry Authority, provincially owned, are building a new tradition along the coast. This is Captain Thomas Parkinson, com- modore and senior master of the 23-vessel fleet, captain of the *Queen of Prince Rupert*, its newest addition. He has navigated the coastal waters 31 years.

8

The Mightiest Resource

S ome parts of British Columbia receive only a few inches of rain a year. Other parts suffer torrential cloudbursts. Even people who live in the latter areas do not realize that the total amount of precipitation falling on the province is 204 trillion gallons a year. That is 560 billion gallons a day. It is an incomprehensible amount, especially when it is realized that the entire United States consumes 315 billion gallons of water daily; and by 1980 will probably need 560 billion gallons – the equivalent of the daily provincial rainfall.

Householders who use about 65 gallons per capita daily are prone to forget that water is not only a necessity of life but necessary in the economics and way of life. For example, it takes 50,000 gallons of water to make a ton of paper, 100,000 gallons to refine a ton of copper, 30,000 gallons to yield one person's lifetime supply of bread, 200,000 gallons to grow a ton of alfalfa, 250 gallons a day to nurture one Douglas fir tree, and 25 gallons to ripen just one ear of corn.

History's most poignant pages recount many tragedies that occurred because man did not conserve this indispensable resource. Whole civilizations have vanished and where once they thrived parched deserts remain. Today's more knowledgeable civilizations, though still improvident, have come to realize that water is not inexhaustible. Many thinking British Columbians have come to agree with conservationists in government and private life that of all the province's riches none is more precious than its abundant supply of fresh water; that it will be the strongest magnet drawing industries and hundreds of thousands of thirsty, water-seeking people in the next half century.

The water surface of the globe is said to be 139.4 million square miles. The 18 principal oceans and seas cover 136.9 million square miles, the 28 main lakes occupy 439.8 thousand square miles, while the 28 chief rivers are in total 68,272 miles long. British Columbia's share of fresh-water lakes is 6,976 square miles. The Fraser River, longest wholly-contained within the province and one of the world's greatest, is 850 miles long. The province contains 466 miles of the Columbia River, mainstay of the northwest United States.

British Columbia is blessed not only by the number and size of its rivers but by the fact its mountain terrain converts otherwise placid water to a foaming, surging force as it seeks the sea. Thus the hydro-electric power potential of the province is vast and limited only for practical pur-

poses because there are not enough sites on the rivers suitable for the installation of dams and turbines. Despite an increase in generating, present-day thinking is that dam construction on the Peace and Columbia rivers should have started two years before it did. The installed hydro-electric power capacity is some 2,660,000 kilowatts and half of it is produced by the British Columbia Hydro and Power Authority. By 1985, the Peace and Columbia river systems will have an installed capacity of 4,090,000 kilowatts. This will raise the provincial total of installed capacity to 6,750,000 kilowatts.

But there may be trouble ahead. In 1961, using a load growth rate of 6.3 percent, compounded annually, the British Columbia Energy Board forecast that 1985's estimated population of three million would need the production of 10 million kilowatts. But instead of a 6.3 percent growth rate, power demand on Hydro since 1955 has increased an average of 10 percent a year, and for the year ending March 31, 1966, the increase was 15.8 percent. As a result, Hydro's engineers now wonder if the growth rate may not average out at 9 percent by 1985. If it does the province will need power additional to the output of the Columbia and Peace river projects. By then, a second plant is expected to be in production about 12 miles downstream from the giant Portage Mountain generating plant on the Peace River. It will be a "run-of-river" plant, which uses the regulated flow of the river at that point to spin its turbines. By 1985, further "run-of-river" sites are expected to be available. Should these sources still prove inadequate to the demand, Hydro engineers may tap the potential of the Iskut and Stikine rivers, halfway up the Alaska

Panhandle, for inclusion into the provincial power grid. Studies have begun on those sites. Then there is the mighty potential of the Fraser River which carves its way from far inland to tidewater at New Westminster. Completed surveys indicate generating plants totalling some six million kilowatts could be installed on the Fraser system, a total that could more than double as power generation research makes more sites economically feasible. Need, economics, and the development of a method to preserve the great salmon runs will determine when and how these sites are developed. In the meantime, Hydro knows now that the winter of 1967 may bring the province's first major importation of power since the Columbia generators may be late in meeting present demands of the burgeoning economy. It will be supplied from systems within the Northwest Power Pool, of which Hydro is a member, and possibly from Alberta.

But what of the present? Of its 1.9 million population, British Columbia has only some 700,000 wage earners. That is less than half the population of metropolitan Toronto. Each of the 700,000 is contributing one thousand dollars to the $700 million first stage cost of the Peace River power development. When this is compared to the $641 million St. Lawrence Seaway project, much of it paid from federal funds, it is no wonder British Columbians are proud, as in summer, they stand by the thousands on the edges of the Peace and watch the great machines thunder in the valley.

From the time the 1.25-mile-long, 600-foot-high gravel, sand and rock dam is completed in 1968 and the water begins backing up, it will take more than two years to fill the reservoir. By that time it will have become the largest lake in British Columbia – 240 miles long, covering 640 square miles. Buried deep in a chiselled cavern in the river's wall on one side of the dam will be the western world's largest underground powerhouse with a generating capacity almost 20 percent greater than the existing Grand Coulee Dam. The entire complex is one of the largest construction projects undertaken anywhere in the world in the sixties. It could never have been started without a fortunate assist from nature. Not only was the site magnificent in terms of dam engineering, but eons ago a retreating glacier had left a moraine only four miles away large enough to provide the necessary 60 million cubic yards of material. This brought into play the world's largest conveyor belt system, costing $10 million. It moves 12,000 tons of gravel an hour and fills an earth-mover dumper truck with 100 tons in 30 seconds.

There is little room at the Peace project for the shovel and wheelbarrow labourer. At peak employment in 1966 and 1967, only 3,300 will be working – not many in view of what is being done. Most men are machine experts and their pay cheques, up to a thousand dollars a month, show it. Contractors building the Hydro transmission lines from the site offer linemen up to two thousand dollars a month which includes the standard pay rate of six hundred dollars, plus all overtime at double time, and free board.

The other part of the simultaneous two-river power development is on the Columbia, where a $500 million complex of three dams and a generating station is being installed. Although 466 miles of the river lie within British Columbia, its remaining 750 miles is in the United States. In return for providing Columbia River water storage in British Columbia for power generation and flood control purposes, the United States has paid British Columbia $273 million and will pay another $70 million over a period of years. The money has been invested and the interest is expected to make up the total sum the province will need to construct the three dams.

First to be finished will be the 6.4 million cubic yard Duncan Dam, costing $33 million. It will be finished in April, 1968. A year later the 8.5 million cubic yard, $129 million Arrow Dam will be finished. Four years after that, in 1973, the Mica Dam will bring the ambitious project to an end. Mica will contain 37 million cubic yards of fill and will be 645 feet high. It will cost $245 million. Unlike the Peace, the Columbia dams will flood some dozen small communities and over 2,000 people are being relocated.

Impressive as these developments may be there still remain within the province hydroelectric sites capable of generating nearly 24 million kilowatts representing 32 million horsepower.

In the Peace and Columbia projects there has arisen the opportunity for the province to buy from countries which are customers for its raw materials. To March, 1966, $63.2 million in foreign contracts were awarded. Of this, $19.6 million went to Japan for turbines and other heavy equipment. England, Switzerland, Sweden, France and Germany were other successful bidders. A Yugoslav firm captured the $5.1 million contract for the foundation treatment under the Peace Dam. Because of the projects, new people bringing their skills have become residents.

100-TON CAPACITY belly-dumper truck moves into position to drop its load of fill at the Peace River damsite. Inset—artist's conception of completed dam showing the powerhouse.

More Men and Determination

No bolder projects involving great feats of engineering are to be seen anywhere in the western world than in British Columbia as it enters its second century. This is especially true of the hydroelectric power projects. They will continue to be a source of amazement for a very long time as the program accelerates to meet demands for industrial power which in the years ahead will be far greater than even the most optimistic forecasts. Here are five photographs serving merely to indicate, not portray, what men and machines, spurred by iron determination and backed by faith and cash, are accomplishing in the mid-sixties. From the wheeled belly-dumpers on the Peace to the belly-splitting barges on the Columbia, it is one vast panorama of progress.

Portage Mountain Dam

OVER THE HILLS AND FAR AWAY snakes the world's longest conveyor belt carrying Peace River Dam fill to the damsite from a glacial moraine some four miles away.

LINEMEN WORK ON TOWERS for new Hydro transmission lines running into Kelly Lake substation, north of Lillooet. The station, run by microwave, is unattended.

SOME 600,000 KILOWATTS is produced by the four generators of Burrard thermal plant near Vancouver. It consumes 130 million cubic feet of natural gas daily.

Duncan Dam   **Arrow Dam**   **Mica Dam**

UNIQUE, BELLY-SPLITTING BARGE surges upward in the water after dropping its load of rock fill in precise location over the site on the Columbia River at Castle-gar where the $8.5 million Arrow Dam will rise to form one of the river's three dams. Inset: an artist's conceptions of dams when all of them are completed.

AT ALCAN, KITIMAT, six pot lines produced over 200,000 tons of aluminum in 1965 for markets around the world

9 Room for Growth

The photograph above is representative of manufacturing in British Columbia. So is the photograph on page 105. This is large-scale, resource-oriented manufacturing. It is very different from the consumer-oriented production of Ontario's industrial belt. Though the province does not produce automobiles, power lawn mowers, corn flakes, cameras, cosmetics or catsup, manufacturing is nevertheless a great force in the economy. In the first half of the sixties, it accounted for a constant 45 to 47 percent of the net value of the entire commodity production. Construction totalled between 20 and 25 percent. The balance consisted of logging, 13 to 16 percent; mining, 4 to 6 percent; electric power, 5 percent; agriculture, 4.5 to 4.9 percent; fishing and trapping, 1.5 to 2 percent. Secondary industries are obviously the backbone of the provincial economy, although much of the manufacturing is of a primary nature.

In 1954, the sales value of factory shipments from all provincial plants totalled $1,474 million. By 1965, that figure had risen to $2,881 million. The wood products industries, including sawmills, shingle mills, pulp and paper mills, plywood and veneer plants, accounted for about half of all factory shipments and for the largest part of new manufacturing plants in recent years. Food and beverages make up about 20 percent of all shipments, followed by the primary metal industries of Trail and Kitimat (10 percent) and metal fabrication, chemical products, and transportation equipment.

The most spectacular feature of the province's industrial scene is the enormous expansion taking place in the pulp and paper industry. In 1960, Prince George was a small sawmilling town. Now there are two pulp mills in operation and a third is being built. Other pulp mills at Kitimat, Prince Rupert, Gold River, Houston, Mackenzie and Skookumchuck will all be in operation by 1972. They will revitalize established communities and in some cases create entirely new ones.

The expansion will have a mighty and widespread effect on other secondary industries. Already, plants producing chemicals almost exclusively for the pulp industry have been constructed at Vancouver, Harmac and Squamish. Caustic and chlorine plants have been proposed for Prince George, Prince Rupert, Crofton and Kitimat. Only a few years ago these vital chemicals were all imported. A million dollar plant to manufacture felts for pulp and paper mills opened recently in North Vancouver. A $4 million truck assembly plant is planned for Kelowna. The forest and mining industries growth means increasing markets for numerous local firms producing machinery, equipment and operating supplies.

In 1965, new capital investment in manufacturing plants amounted to $312 million. For 1966 it is expected to be $365 million. This is more than the new plant investment of Alberta, Saskatchewan, Manitoba, New Brunswick, Nova Scotia, Newfoundland and Prince Edward Island combined. During 1966, more than half of all the outlay for manufacturing plants, machinery and equipment was in the paper and allied industries. A distant second will be the wood products plants with a total investment of $65 million. Food and beverage plants will account for $23 million. Remaining capital outlay for 1966 will be $19 million in chemical product manufacturing facilities, $13 million for petroleum and coal products, $6 million for metal fabricating and $3 million for transportation equipment. These figures illustrate the need that exists in the province for secondary manufacturing to build a stronger economic base.

Rapid industrial growth has been accompanied, and even exceeded, by growth in the support industries. They employ more than 65 percent of the labour force compared with about 25 percent in manufacturing and construction. Some of these firms manufacture services, not commodities. One of the largest is Canadian Pacific Airlines.

CPA has the distinction of being one of the largest concerns with international connections that is based in Vancouver, where 1,800 of its 1,900 employees live and work. The company's payroll is some $13 million annually, most of which, together with about $9 million in operating expenses, is distributed in the province. By way of comparison, Alcan Ltd., at Kitimat, the sole support of that northern community of 10,000, has since the start of aluminum smelting there in 1954, injected an average of $22.2 million a year into the provincial economy in the form of wages, purchases and taxes.

Another airline is Pacific Western Airlines, also based in Vancouver. After Air Canada and CPA, it is Canada's third largest. In 1965, its gross revenue was $11.5 million.

In addition to the promising outlook for forestry and mining, the abundant supply of power now on the horizon will be the next most important factor in determining the strength and direction of the province's industrial development. It may bring a needed smelter and that would soon be followed by growth in metal fabricating industries.

Apart from the primary manufacturing industries, the processing of wood, fish, ores and farm produce, what of secondary manufacturing? On the whole, it is small and serves either the primary industries or the local consumer, though a number of industries do export. Only when lower transportation costs are a factor in securing sales abroad, or when items made locally are not made elsewhere, do secondary manufacturers now produce primarily for export from the province.

British Columbia has good highways and a tidewater location but transportation costs are high. Tariff walls tend to discourage export to nearby coast markets in the United States, while the local population is not large enough to warrant mass production of most goods. The province thus looks to the Pacific rim countries, principally Japan, for the sale of its industrial products and the future of its consumer industries. Until such time as underdeveloped Pacific rim countries have the purchasing power to buy products of secondary manufacturing industries, local expansion will be governed largely by the needs of western Canada.

These problems are somewhat unique to British Columbia. One difficulty it shares with many is the inflationary spiral of high living costs and high wages. This becomes most important to the province when it is combined with the other factors of limited markets and high transportation costs. Local industrial leaders believe union leaders' wage demands result in a cost-price squeeze for many manufacturers. They say the squeeze is causing some firms to turn more and more to automation while others have to cut back on local production and increase imports. They hold that British Columbia's conditions make a co-operative labour-management approach more important than elsewhere.

In any case, with the provincial population expected to be 2.3 million by 1975, sheer weight of numbers will result in gains in consumer-oriented industrial production. There will certainly be a similar pattern of growth in the neighbouring provinces and American states and it is anticipated that local business will benefit. As the population increases, improvements are made in transportation, and the standards of living elsewhere rise toward the level now enjoyed by most British Columbians, the cost factors inhibiting consumer manufacturing are expected to decrease in importance.

Skilled Labour

In company with most of the western world, British Columbia is experiencing a serious manpower shortage. Indications are that it will worsen before it gets better. By 1970 it is known now that an additional 4,000 skilled men will be needed by the pulp and paper industry alone. Mines need 1,000 hard-rock men right now. As automation of forest, mine and factory becomes more universal, it means that if a man is not to be replaced by a machine, he must master the technique of running one. Where are the trained, the skilled, the ambitious and the adventuresome coming from to meet the challenge of rising demand that is already here?

"GREEN CHAIN" at Weldwood of Canada Ltd., Vancouver, where thin veneer comes off lathe and is graded by the off-bearers before being dried and laminated.

SHIPBUILDING (right) at yards in Victoria and Vancouver is part of traditional coast life. Here at Victoria Machinery Depot another *Queen* ferry takes shape.

FULL-BODIED PURPLE GRAPES move to the crusher at Kelowna from nearby Okanagan vineyards to become part of a million-dollar-a-year wine-making industry.

SUPER-PRECISE MANUFACTURING is this production at Trail of 99.999999999 percent pure gold for space-age electronics. Thalium, indium, antimony are others.

10

Building Human Resources

When the Hudson's Bay Company's annual supply vessel *Columbia* dropped anchor off Fort Victoria in 1849, it brought Anglican Rev. R. J. Staines from Northamptonshire, England, to be the colony's first schoolteacher. He was paid a hundred pounds as the Fort's chaplain, 340 pounds as teacher, 40 pounds to hire a servant.

From this beginning, British Columbia has developed an education system as comprehensive and modern as any in Canada. Indicative of the progress that has been made is 1965's report of the Canadian Economic Council which stated that the educational level of the provincial labour force was the highest in the country. This fact is directly related to the Council's statement that average earned income per employed person in British Columbia between 1960 and 1964, was 19 percent above the national average. It substantiates the doctrine of the sixties that prosperity depends on productivity, that productivity varies directly in relation to the educational level of the population.

From the time Staines opened his first little school, to the passage of the Free Public School Act in 1872 when public administration of education really began, the number of students in the colony grew to 400. In the 1966 school year they exceeded 420,000. Some 16,200 teachers, whose qualifications as a teaching corps surpass on the average those of any other province, staff 1,400 schools with a pupil population ranging from 2,000-plus in the metropolitan areas to less than ten in some elementary schools in more remote parts. A centralization of the higher grades is taking place. Elementary grades are taught in more than 1,300 schools but the senior secondary grades of 11 and 12 are taught in only 170 schools. Brought about partly as a result of better highways and the installation of an extensive school bus system, centralization allows children from small communities and isolated ranches to take advantage of the wider, better opportunities offered by the larger schools.

In the process, one of life's little tragedies is often enacted. When a youngster has outgrown the facilities in his own rural school district he must say good-bye to his moist-eyed parents and leave for a larger centre. He may live in one of the province's 10 school dormitories in such places as the Gulf Islands, Kamloops, 100-Mile House and Vanderhoof where students board at nominal cost under the eye of qualified matrons. For others to whom even dormitories are too far away, the Department of Education operates a complete correspondence school program to Grade 13. The service is available to British Columbians abroad, to physically handicapped children at home, and to men and women ambitious to raise their educational level. In 1966, some 19,000 students were served by correspondence.

While the province leads Canada in the number of teachers holding university degrees, in company with the rest of the continent it has a shortage of fully-qualified teachers at the secondary level. Ultimately the Department of Education wants all teachers to have a university degree.

Since 1960, British Columbia's public school curriculum has been revised completely. It is now abreast of modern, pedagogic science, enabling graduates to meet the demands of a rapidly changing social and technological society. Although the revision begins in the elementary grades, the impact is most forceful in Grades 11 and 12. Here, since 1965, students have had a choice of six employment-oriented courses of study. Previously, they had only two choices: a university entrance or a general program. Many fell victim to their or their parents' desire for a university program for prestige reasons rather than considering first their own ability and interests, and many failed. While still concerned with the fundamentals of general education, the new programs encourage students and parents to recognize that not all have the same talents. The academic-technical program qualifies those who graduate for entry to a university or to the Institute of Technology. The others, commerce, industry, community service, fine arts, and the last category, "training for particular occupations," lead directly to employment or, preferably, to further and more specialized training at a vocational school or a community college.

As the province's long-range plans to establish secondary industry and to convert the natural resources into wealth got under way in the 1950's, it was soon apparent that skilled labour was the key to progress. A means was provided in 1961 with the signing of the Federal-Provincial Technical and Vocational Training Agreement. Vocational schools, the next step for many secondary school students who graduate on the vocational programs, now exist in Vancouver, Burnaby, Nanaimo,

Nelson, Kelowna, Prince George, Dawson Creek and Victoria. A new school is to be built at Victoria to replace existing rented quarters. Other new ones are going up at Kamloops and Terrace. Schools of Art at Nelson and Vancouver are part of the system. The vocational schools offer pre-apprenticeship training in the indentured trades, pre-employment training, trades-extension training and general upgrading.

Not always understood are the boundaries between trades training and technological training. In general, a technician supervises the application of a professional's theory, translating it in terms of a tradesman's work. In a developing province where the practical application of technology is the measure of industrial success, he is the essential specialist requiring education that is balanced between the theoretical and the practical. This he finds at the Institute of Technology at Burnaby which graduated its first 2-year students in 1966. Already, the school is being enlarged. By 1970 it will graduate 1,600 students a year in 27 separate technologies ranging from instrumentation and control to medical radiology, electronics and broadcast communications.

Like other places of learning the Institute is open at night for working men and women. Technicians presently employed attend in hundreds to upgrade their skills to qualify, like the day students, for a nationally acceptable certificate of technology. There is now a realization that as man's store of knowledge doubles every 10 years, education is no longer terminal and confined to the early years. In 1966, some 140,000 British Columbians — one out of every seven eligible adults — who had completed formal training and were still under age 60, were back at school.

Vancouver's night school enrolment alone is an astronomically high 38,000. Courses include all school grades and vocational and technological courses but also offer subjects such as Job Hunting Techniques, How to Use Consumer Credit Wisely, and How to Play Par Golf!

One Institute of Technology will not satisfy the needs of a province whose ribbon of development follows a twisted pattern, 1500 miles long. A new kind of institution, the community college, is satisfying the need. It offers the first two years of a general university academic program together with a 2-year technical program comparable to that at the Burnaby Institute. The first such college opened in Vancouver in 1965. The second, Selkirk College at Castlegar in the Kootenays, opened in 1966. A third will be ready in the Okanagan in the autumn of 1968. Others are being considered for central Vancouver Island, the Fraser Valley and the central interior. They are set up under the provisions of the Public Schools Act. Although new, already there is evidence they will exercise a significant influence on the general educational level. They will relieve the crowding of first year university classes and as well, by making university training available closer to home, they will eventually increase the number of degree-holding graduates. In addition, they will allow non-university students to obtain technical training at a higher level than before. In general, enrolment will be open to all those who have graduated from the secondary school programs. Community colleges will serve also as local centres for vocational and cultural development to an extent and degree not available previously in most of the areas where they will be built. They will be able to offer courses in a wide variety of fields to adults seeking further knowledge.

Meanwhile, British Columbia's three public universities and the private university at Nelson are expanding rapidly in anticipation of the numbers of students that are expected from a growing population and a broadened educational exposure. University of British Columbia, all alone until less than a decade ago, had more than 17,000 students in 1966 on its sea-view Point Grey campus, west of Vancouver. University of Victoria, a junior college until 1963, now building a magnificent campus at Gordon Head, north of Victoria, had more than 3,400 students. Simon Fraser University, an acropolis of modern architecture on the top of Burnaby Mountain, east of Vancouver, opened in 1965 with 2,500 students. It was Canada's first university to incorporate the tri-semester system. It conducts its classes year-round. In the 1966-67 fiscal year the provincial government is providing $25 million as its share of the operating expenses the three public universities and $8 million more for capital expenses. UBC is undergoing a $13 million expansion covering 1,000 acres. Among the additions to its campus: buildings for dentistry, music, forestry-agriculture and a new sports stadium.

In the 1966-67 fiscal year, the Department of Education will spend the biggest piece of the budget – $167 million. When the first Public School Act was implemented in 1872, the initial budget provided was $40,000. The story of education in 1966 is a far cry from those days. But what price education when it is compared in value to the abundant wealth it creates.

UNIVERSITY OF BRITISH COLUMBIA at Vancouver has over 17,000 attending; does more pure post-graduate research than any other in Western Canada; attracts students from 60 countries. Here in the Physics Department, the Van de Graaff nuclear accelerator is set up for a new experiment.

A Wide Variety of Facilities

From the startling mall of Simon Fraser University (page 106) to the log-walled veranda of a trader's house at Germansen Landing (page 115) it is 450 air miles but they are linked by the common thirst for knowledge and education that is now flooding over British Columbia in a wave of ever-freshening force. With so many facilities, no student need any longer enter his working life untrained or unfit. Business and industry can expect job applicants to have some measure of knowledge of their operation. It is as H. G. Wells said in 1920 in his *Outline of History*: "Human history becomes more and more a race between education and catastrophe."

KUMSHEEN SECONDARY SCHOOL at Lytton, opened 1962, is typical of hundreds of modern B.C. schools. This one, with 150 students, has 65 percent Indian enrolment.

WELDING CLASS is one of many such practical courses offered by provincial vocational schools like this one at Burnaby. Most graduates will find jobs awaiting.

UNIVERSITY OF VICTORIA on Vancouver Island is building a completely new campus at Gordon Head, site of a wartime officers' training camp. Once affiliated with the University of British Columbia, it is now independent. This is the $3.2 million library. It will seat 1,000 at study and it houses 315,000 books.

SCHOOL DORMITORY at Lillooet is one of several in province run by Department of Education for school children whose homes are beyond daily bus routes.

SCHOOL AT LILLOOET is typical of the new schools being built all over B.C.This one combines elementary and secondary grades requiring a total of 27 teachers.

NIGHT SCHOOLS are packed with adults intent on improvement. These are new Canadians learning English in Vancouver where attendance is Canada's highest.

GRADE 9 CORRESPONDENCE STUDENT Keith Westfall, 14, is one of three in his trading post family acquiring education by mail at Germansen Landing in Omineca.

VANCOUVER'S WEST END,
city's oldest residential
area, is being rejuvenated
by a high-rise apartment
development unlike any-
thing in the city's history.
The towers seen here have
all been built since 1961.

II

The Social Scene is Changing

W hen the British Columbian chooses a place to live he faces challenge again, because he has an abundant choice of living and working environment. Whatever his tastes and his talents, he can find a place to suit his needs and aspirations. If he is a loner there are places so remote he could spend the rest of his life in solitude. If bright lights are his desire, there are cosmopolitan cities. He can choose between moist climate or dry climate, moderate temperature or one of extremes. He can live by the sea or high on a mountain. He can surround himself with tall timber or stand deep in the grass of the flatlands. It is up to him. All he has to do is choose. In the choosing he has helped start many small communities that didn't exist a decade ago.

The simplest form of local organization is called an improvement district. It can be set up to provide one or more services like water supply or fire protection to a group of people in a designated area. When 500 people have gathered, they may form a village and elect representatives to regulate their affairs. After another 2,000 arrive, the village may become a town and accept additional powers and the responsibility for social welfare. It may become a city when the population reaches 5,000. Then one of its added charges will be the provision of police protection. Most British Columbia communities outside

Victoria and Vancouver have set up contractual agreements with the Royal Canadian Mounted Police to handle their police work. The RCMP also serves as the provincial police force.

In 1965, two pieces of legislation were passed which indicate the changing demands of community living. One of them permitted the birth of "instant towns." These miracles of mid-sixty technology, complete with shopping centre, theatre, community hall, and good houses with all the modern amenities are set up in the wilderness, usually, to service a nearby mining or forest enterprise. The other legislation recognized that the automobile has changed the old concept of a single, close-knit community into a concept of several smaller ones forming a trading area with one or more defined centres. For these the act permits the formation of a local organization called a regional district. This makes it possible for several single communities to form a regional board for the co-ordination of over-all planning of water supply, recreational facilities, air and water pollution, hospitals, inspection services and other such facilities. In this way more and better amenities are provided at less cost than a single community would pay. Eventually the province is expected to have 23 regional districts super-imposed on the 32 cities, eight towns, 59 villages and 34 district municipalities existing in British Columbia on March 1, 1966.

Despite the abundant variety of hearths and homes, more than two-thirds of the province's population has chosen to live on the lower half of Vancouver Island and the south-west corner of the mainland which includes Vancouver and the Fraser Valley as far east as Hope. This is where history and geography dictated the British Columbian concentrate his commercial and industrial endeavours, and concentrate he has. Nevertheless, within that comparatively small area the people live in a wide variety of environments that allow full scope for the expression of individuality – a rite that is almost a religion in the entire Pacific Northwest. The man who lives on a rock over the sea with a view to the horizon can't understand the one who resides among trees so tall it is shady at noon. The one with a big garden has no envy for the penthouse dweller life-lined by an elevator. "To each his own" is an apt phrase, for there is an intense pride of ownership wherever he lives, whatever he does. This holds equally for his boat, his city, his club and his wife – although the province's divorce rate is Canada's highest.

What of the cities? Much that is worthy has risen despite inhibiting restrictions demanding public mandates for many development plans. These in turn allow the opponents of change to organize their disapproval. More than once, in past years, Vancouver has been called "a site in search of a city." More recently, it has been called "a city in search of a heart," referring to the seemingly interminable wrangling over two ancient city blocks whose redevelopment will mark the rejuvenation of the downtown shopping section. The west end, 1910's better home district and until recently a tired drab of wooden boarding houses, between the city centre and Stanley Park, is undergoing a spectacular transformation. Spire after balconied spire of high-rise apartments stand row on row. One is 32 storeys high. These, with some tall, new downtown office buildings and some housing developments in the suburbs, have accounted for $300 million worth of construction since 1963. New construction amounted to $240 million of that total. Almost overnight it seems, the city has acquired an exciting skyline that shimmers in the western sunset. At last Vancouver has begun to look like Canada's third city should.

Another new skyline is thrusting up along the shore line of West Vancouver, the municipality across Lion's Gate Bridge from the city proper. In the 1930's, "West Van" consisted of a single row of seashore cottages between the rocks and Marine Drive. It was linked to the city by a faithful little ferry which battled manfully with the fast tidal currents of First Narrows. Those who lived there were thought "different." The bridge brought expansion to the mountainside. Its present population of 31,500 grew by 10,000 in the first five years of the sixties. A Vancouver bedroom with no industry, until 1960 the area was entirely single-family dwellings. There were 5,400 school children. Since then, new zoning bylaws have permitted 35 apartments to be built. The school enrollment is 8,100. By 1975, it is expected to be 10,200 with a corresponding rise in property taxes to pay for the five new schools needed, plus major additions to present facilities. The British Properties' fine residential development opened up more of its mountainside holdings in 1966 and before the $15,000 lots were ready there was a long waiting list. Stretching over 12 miles to Horseshoe Bay on Howe Sound, West Vancouver homes have won more national architectural awards than any other residential area in Canada. The municipality contains about 1,000 of metropolitan Vancouver's estimated 3,000 private swimming pools.

In a very similar fashion West Van's sister community of North Vancouver, suburban Burnaby, the Fraser River delta areas of Surrey and Richmond, the Fraser Valley cities and towns like Langley and Chilliwack, are all undergoing expansion and face-lifting. The latter are better able to cope with local problems since the new Trans-Canada Highway passes outside their limits instead of through their centres as formerly. New Westminster managed to secure the unanimous co-operation of the merchants lining Columbia Street to install new lighting and rock-faced planter boxes. The blocks-long and multi-tiered parking ramp behind the stores has instilled a busy air into that historic port on the Fraser River.

Despite the tour spielers, hawkers, bagpipers, old London double-decker buses and tallyhos assembled in front of Victoria's gracefully aging Empress Hotel to attract tourists hoping to catch a glimpse of Olde England, Olde England is no more. Only here and there do the sight-seers catch a wisp of Victoria Past. Victoria Present no longer fusty, is fast changing its traditional facade. Things seem to be still in the same old places, but there is a difference. A $7 million Centennial Museum and Archives complex is taking shape between the hotel and the Parliament Buildings, which will house among other things, the world's finest collection of Pacific Northwest Indian art. The gay-nineties City Hall on Douglas Street still stands. It has been freshened and enlarged with a modern addition. Now linked with refurbished MacPherson

Playhouse and other new and reconstructed buildings, the grouping adjoins an astonishingly fountained plaza. Called Centennial Square, it has brought zest to a once-languishing block. Beacon Hill Park, still lovely, has been fenced on the west by modern, balconied apartments. Between Centennial Square and the park, tall, glass-fronted office buildings add sparkle to the downtown business area. Even the sedate bedroom municipality of Oak Bay, east of the city, has been transformed by a dozen new waterfront apartments. An extensive marina development includes a quality restaurant and an undersea marine garden. To the west, in Esquimalt, the Royal Canadian Navy's western base stands ready as it has for more than a century. The Navy's ships are larger, sleeker, faster and more complex but the 5,000 men who man and maintain them are as much a part of the community of Greater Victoria as they ever were.

British Columbia's most northern coastal city is Prince Rupert, a major seaport. It is not as remote now as it was when connected only by rail to the east. The new provincial ferry service from Vancouver Island took 20,000 tourists to the city during its first summer of operation in 1966. Some continued on to Alaska but many headed east on Highway 16 to Prince George, following the banks of the Skeena River past Terrace, a modern little town that forms the gateway to Kitimat, a few miles south. In Prince George, almost the exact geographic heart of the province, they found a fast-paced western boom town with all the traditional worries of a doubling population, high rent for mediocre accommodation, bulging

trailer communities, and other ills that stem from too-sudden growth. The expansion was not hard to see. New pulp mills, new construction, new shopping centres and a new up-to-date hotel occupy the historic site that bears promise of becoming a major city within a decade.

From Prince George, some of the summer tourists followed the Hart Highway north to the Peace River country to see the Peace Dam construction. Those who turned south came to Quesnel and Williams Lake, cattle towns historically, but now enjoying bustling economies brought about by the burgeoning pulp, plywood and lumber industries. South to Kamloops they saw a second city across the Thompson River from the older part. They found a little architectural gem of a new city hall, new department stores and shopping centres, a quality residential section on what used to be a gophered sand hill overlooking the junction of the two rivers, new industries and a new outlook that resulted from the completion of the Rogers Pass road link to Calgary. When the Yellowhead Highway is finished soon, linking Kamloops with Edmonton, Kamloops' bounce will be even higher. Once dependent on the cattle industry, Kamloops now has a pulp mill and further expansion of wood processing is planned, as is more secondary industry, and a half-million-dollar sports centre. In the decade to 1965, the area doubled its population.

Moving southward into the Okanagan Valley, the travellers found Vernon only outwardly its tree-lined old self. A sleek, two-block community centre opened in 1966 and with its new apartment buildings and stores, and a growing share of the winter sports bonanza, there was all the evidence of youthful vitality. Down the lake-hugging road a little, Kelowna's Barnard Avenue was bustling from one end to the other. The travellers found a new city centre, a new vocational school, a new college expected, new secondary industries moving in and the possibility of a large mining operation just over the hill. At the south end of the lake, Penticton's miles of bright motels and trailer courts reminded them of some California towns. They also saw benefits derived from a well-organized tourist and fruit industry.

Down further to Osoyoos then east into the Kettle Valley and the Kootenays, past the smoking chimneys of the Trail smelters, they followed a superb highway to Castlegar where a pulp mill, the Arrow Dam construction, and a regional college have awakened the Columbia River town. They found Nelson more a mixture of the old and the new than ever with the chestnut trees, the good homes that climb the banks of the lake and the silver-rush architecture of the city hall forming vivid contrast to the modern campus of Notre Dame University. Further east they found Kimberley and Cranbrook, viable and hustling and like the rest of the province, awake to a hungry world's need for their wood products and minerals.

T hose are some of the established places that began life as trading posts or were born around the turn of the century because of a mineral find or, in the case of the Okanagan cities, because watering the desert made good farm land. But now there are other places the tourist does not see so readily. They are the instant towns tucked away in the wild country, born of immediate need, planned on a drawing board to infinite

degree, traditionless. They are financed by large companies with interests in the area, who then turn the new towns over to the worker-citizens to manage.

Ten years ago, Gold River, at the head of Muchalat Inlet running deep inland from the west coast of Vancouver Island, was a timber camp that supplied logs for the mill at Tahsis in the next inlet. In 1964, an East Asiatic Company pulp mill was authorized and by the summer of 1966 an instant town was rising rapidly. As the year was ending, 200 loggers and 1,100 construction workers were on the site. Of these, 65 men had installed their young families in permanent, urban-type houses and there were another 50 in the trailer compound. One school had opened and another will be ready for the 1967 school year. The installed services are based on an expected population of 5,000.

Port McNeill on the northeast coast of Vancouver Island, across the channel from Alert Bay, was a logging company site for a number of years until it became a village in 1966. In 1963, there was one car and one telephone for a population of 450. By the fall of 1966, there were 400 cars and 285 telephones for 1,000 people.

In 1955, Hudson's Hope was a settlement of 25 people on the Peace River. By 1965, with the impact of the Portage Mountain Dam construction, the population numbered 3,241 and there were 35 enterprises with a volume of $2.4 million.

These are some, but by no means all. As much as the gardens of Victoria and the commerce of Vancouver, they represent the environmental variety of life in British Columbia. Visitors seeing the newer towns for the first time wish they were 20 years younger and able to share in the big years ahead.

THERE ARE SOME WHO SAY the old statue of the young Queen Victoria in front of the Parliament Buildings, Victoria (above) has a twinkle in her eyes now as she quietly watches the changes in her namesake city. At right is newly-created Centennial Square with its mosaic fountain, plaza and a new complex of old City Hall (left) addition (right) and McPherson Theatre.

Communities of Spirit

The Parliament Buildings' bronze likeness of Queen Victoria is a strangely modern symbol. From the provincial capital, across the cities, towns and wilderness trading posts, to the inlet-hidden float villages (page 131) youthfulness has energized the Big Country where determination and confidence prevail. The old but youthful statue uniquely stands now, as it did in the past, for the singular spirit that charges the atmosphere wherever people are forging their communities.

PORT ALBERNI, and amalgamating sister city of Alberni, at the head of west coast Vancouver Island's Alberni Inlet, is major seaport for shipment of paper, lumber.

NEW WESTMINSTER, the mainland's oldest city, is a busy port on the Fraser River. New riverside car parking ramps can be seen here, just left of centre in photo.

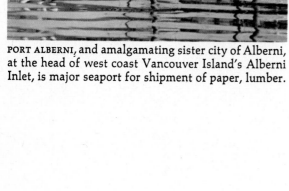

WEST VANCOUVER shore, looking east to Lion's Gate and Vancouver harbour, is giving way to more high-rise apartments, replacing seaside cottages of the 1930's.

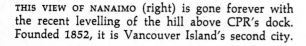

THIS VIEW OF NANAIMO (right) is gone forever with the recent levelling of the hill above CPR's dock. Founded 1852, it is Vancouver Island's second city.

KELOWNA (above), a few miles north of Penticton on Okanagan Lake, is the fruit capital of the province. Its name derives from the Indian for "grizzly bear."

PENTICTON at the south end of Okanagan Lake, surrounded by orchards, gets only 10 inches of rain a year, more hours of summer sunshine than Honolulu.

KAMLOOPS (below), at the junction of 3 main provincial highways, is the hub city of an inland empire that grows in major resources development every year.

VERNON (below), at the north end of Okanagan Lake, remembered by thousands who took wartime training there, still maintains its main street shade trees.

PRINCE GEORGE, at the junction of the Nechako and Fraser rivers, is the commercial and transportation centre of B.C.'s central interior. It began in 1808 when Simon Fraser established a trading post. Three great new pulp and paper mills have begun an industrial era that may well double present population by 1969.

DAWSON CREEK, Mile Zero of the Alaska Highway, is experiencing a boom through petroleum development. Area also ships two million bushels of grain annually.

TRAIL, because of the Cominco smelters, is called the city of lead and zinc. It is a melting pot of nationalities. It is divided into two parts by Columbia River.

NELSON, on Kootenay Lake, was result of the silver boom of 1896. It was laid out in 1897. Many fine examples of the architecture of that period still remain.

PRINCE RUPERT, with the continuing improvement of Highway 16 from Prince George and the ferry link with Vancouver Island, has become a tourist centre.

KYUQUOT Indian village on Kyuquot Sound on the west coast of Vancouver Island might be any one of a hundred such villages strung along its full length.

GERMANSEN LANDING, a northern interior trading post where Germansen Creek meets the Omineca River, is populated by Westfall family, gets mail once a month.

TAHSIS (left) is a company-created-and-maintained sawmilling centre on Vancouver Island's west coast with a population of 1,200, of whom 450 are workmen.

LOGGERS' FLOATING VILLAGE off Rivers Inlet is home to 20 adults and children. Typical of some 300 such coast "villages," it moves to new locations as jobs change.

12

Leisure and Time to Spend it

One comment often made about the people of the Pacific coast from Tijuana, Mexico, to Prince Rupert is that they play as hard as they work. There may be some truth in it as there is in two apt quotations. Anatole France wrote: "Man is so made that he can only find relaxation from one kind of labour by taking up another." In 1876, Harvard professor John Dwight questioned: "Is not true leisure one with true toil?" The latter is the case in British Columbia where most recreational activities are of the participating kind. With the exception of the spectator sports such as professional football – and at Empire Stadium fans bleed with their B.C. Lions – British Columbians in- dulge themselves with keen personal in- volvement the year round. Most of the outdoor activities are physically arduous and hold a degree of risk.

The fast tides, variable winds, heavy seas, fog and half-submerged deadhead logs make sailboating and power cruising pastimes for the watchful. The corrosive action of sea water and salty atmosphere on paint and metal makes boat-keeping a constant, costly battle of maintenance . . . Mountaineering demands top physical conditioning plus determination and a mind alert to every vagary of a capricious nature, and even a quiet nature walk is sometimes not without minor perils like the spines of the poisonous devil's club shrub or the flesh-burrowing ticks which occasionally infest the grasslands . . . The best trout fishing is inevitably found at the back of beyond, reached only by the hardy packing in on foot, by bush plane or over jeep trails carved on the canyon wall, and for steelhead fishing, toughness is as essential as the rod and line. The mighty, sea-going rainbow trout is a winter fish that returns from the ocean to fight his way as far as 500 miles inland, and attains a size as great as 36 pounds – the weight of the Kispiox River's world-record catch. To take him, fishermen in fleece-lined coats slide down icy rock walls to stand in chest-waders in the freezing water . . . Hunting for big game demands peak physical condition – toughness to stand a cold, above-the-tree-line camp life, to spend hours in a trail saddle, to pack the trophy back to camp over miles of rough country . . . Scuba diving to wrestle an octopus from its lair under fifty feet of cold, green water takes bravery, a strong constitution and complete subjugation of the natural fear that affects those who would explore the unknown . . . Skiing in British Columbia is skiing as it was meant to be – miles-long runs down high, tricky mountain slopes that call for an element of professionalism for the sake of personal safety . . . Even the man who walks no farther than his own garden to find his recreation has a fight on his hands if he lives on the verdant coast. He is forever pulling out and chopping off, battling fungi and mildew, bugs and slugs. The latter are mucous little monsters, black and snail-like, that slip along on their slime at night choosing the youngest annuals in tenderest leaf. They are unique to the coast . . . So it is that in British Columbia leisure and toil can mean the same thing.

The challenge of abundance in the choice of playtime activities available within the province's 366,000 square miles is as apparent as it is in the variety of natural resources. With the number of work-week hours lessening there is more time for recreation. Winter and summer, the problem is what to do first, what to do best and what to do most. The ultimate choice or choices – and there are usually two or three – is based principally on the person's physical state, the available time and the amount of fun-dollars left after the cost of living has taken its toll.

There are an estimated 100,000 salt-water sports fishermen on the coast, some 200,000 resident trout fishermen and there are perhaps another 150,000 tourists who fish either salt or fresh water. The figures increase about 10 percent a year. If all the money spent on boats, trailers, motors, trolling rods and reels, fly rods and reels, lures and other equipment was totalled it would pay for much of the national debt! Fishermen pay a high price per pound for the fish they catch, but fun is immeasurable and when a 40-pound spring salmon, a solid streak of pure muscle, flashes away with 200 feet of taut line, the cost of the fun is worthwhile. Many communities hold annual fishing derbies and the two largest are daily newspaper promotions. Victoria's *Colonist* sponsors one of the world's largest and in some respects it is unique. Each year for six months fishermen work Vancouver Island waters for coho, spring and tyee salmon, lake trout, river trout and steelhead, small-mouthed bass. Monthly and final prizes are awarded in all categories. The highest number of entries so far has been 36,000. Vancouver's *Sun* sponsors the world's largest one-day salmon derby. Some years it attracts as many as 20,000 anglers in 8,000 boats to a 30-square-mile area of saltchuck in Howe Sound. Salmon fishermen, whether in a derby or alone in a boat at dawn, are dedicated, patient people. The reward is the feel of a 60-pound tyee on a trolled piece of herring, or a 14-pound fighting-mad coho on a bucktail fly behind a six-pound test leader. Equally dedicated is the freshwater fisherman who, wading a stream or braving wild winter water is expectant every second for the quick tug that preludes a fight with a rainbow. The *British Columbia Digest*, a Quesnel-published outdoors magazine, said of the rainbow, which is caught from pan to steelhead size: "He is a rootin' tootin' western roughneck with more charm than a pinto pony and the guts and speed of a quarter horse. He's a gaudy gypsy, an aristocratic blue-blood with the growth rate of a Brahma bull and the carefree attitude of an old-time cowpoke." There are his cousins too: Kamloops, cutthroat, brown trout, Dolly Varden, gray fish and lake trout – fighters all.

A lot of fishing is done from boats. An old coast joke with more grim truth than humour is that a boat is a hole in the water lined with wood into which money is pumped. No accurate statistics are available but it has been estimated that the number of pleasure boats in the coastal waters is about 40,000. They would represent a probable value of about $150 million. There is an increase each year. There are 15 marinas in the Vancouver area alone, a dozen around Victoria, many more the length of the coast. The largest in western Canada, mooring some 1,200 boats, is at Fisherman's Cove on the West Vancouver shore. It shelters craft worth in total about $2 million. Some 40 of them

are 40-footers. A 32-foot cruiser which sleeps six may cost as much as $30,000. To this is added another $1,000 a year for insurance, moorage, spring conditioning and painting. After that, add $25 running expenses for each weekend cruise. When the boat bug bites and a man starts trying on yachting caps, the crafty wife will suggest chartering a boat for two weeks instead. At about $50 a day (some charters include a skipper) it is cheaper than owning a boat and having to maintain it all year. For the inexperienced, it is safer, for each year brings its lists of deaths by drowning, explosion, fire and sinking. The Air-Sea Rescue Co-ordination Centre is on constant "red alert."

For those who scorn wall-to-wall comforts such as a range, refrigerator, shower and complete head, and who sail for the expertise it demands, there are the sailboats. Sailors are worse addicts than fishermen or golfers and they snort at the "stink pot" group as they refer to power boaters. They race in many competitive events. The annual Swiftsure classic is the big one, a spring weekend run into the open sea from Victoria. Wind, wave and tide combine awesomely some years to make the 136-nautical-mile race one of the continent's toughest. Usually, there are some provincial boats in the biennial San Francisco-Honolulu Trans-Pacific race. For it crews practise months to attain a ballet-like precision. At least two or three times a year news stories appear about families, or groups of young men, or, as in one case, one man and several girls, outbound for Suva or the Marquesas for a year in the south Pacific, or around the world under sail. In the summer of 1966, there was one Vancouver man who departed his house for a weekend's sailing alone. A long time afterward his wife had a phone call from him, telling her to sell the house and join him. He was in Honolulu. Most of the sea-going jaunters sail heavy ketches and many of them are self-built. In the Van-couver-Victoria area the number of home-built boats far exceeds the number built in shipyards and the whine of power tools and the smell of glue surrounds hundreds of garages, lean-to's and sheds.

There are many who sail on Saturday and then ski on Sunday on slopes that look down upon the water they have sailed. There are 30 developed ski areas and some of them have good resort accom-modation. Of the 30, Vancouver Island has three. Six are on the Lower Mainland, nine in the southern interior, eight in the Kootenays and four are in the north. Thir-teen of them are classed as major ski areas. There are about 70 tows ranging from rope tows, T-bars and Poma lifts to Grouse Mountain's new 50-passenger twin gon-dola lift close to Vancouver. By 9 a.m., on Saturdays and Sundays, thousands of Vancouver skiers have packed the Grouse and Seymour mountain slopes above the city, and thousands who tarried are turned away. Mount Baker, in the state of Wash-ington, a three-hour drive, gets the over-flow and thousands of Canadian skiers have become one of that area's principal sources of income. A new area has been developed at Mount Whistler in Garibaldi Park, a four-hour drive from Vancouver. It resulted from studies made when a strong but unsuccessful attempt was launched to have the 1967 winter Olympic Games in the province. Other good runs are at Green Mountain, just inland from Nanaimo on Vancouver Island, and the Forbidden Plateau near the Island town of Courtenay. Prince George is an enthusias-tic skiing town in the interior, and Nelson, where the Canadian national ski team trains, is a hotbed. So is Kimberley. One of the reasons for all this activity is that parts of the province have almost a patent on perfect powder snow laid on perfect mountain slopes.

For hunters, British Columbia is one of the last frontiers in North America – even better than Alaska. The province is the only place in the world with five varieties of wild sheep: Fannin, Stone, California Bighorn, Rocky Mountain Bighorn and the Dall. There are both mountain and Osborn caribou. Moose are more abun-dant than anywhere else on the continent, and several kinds of deer thrive. Elk herds are increasing. The world's largest grizzly bears live along the coast from Jervis Inlet to Prince Rupert. In other areas, brown, black, and silver-tipped bears flourish. The coast bears do not hibernate in winter because the climate is so mild. By law, every two non-resident hunters must have a licenced guide. He will probably be a Class B guide who works for a Class A guide. The latter is the contractor for the hunting party and charges about $100 per man per day. He supplies horses, tents, utensils, food – everything except a hunt-er's personal gear and weapons. A 12-man shoot will require about 35 pack and saddle horses which are taken into the guide's hunting area in August. Usually, they are out by late October when it gets bitingly cold and uncomfortable. A 10-man sheep hunt in a better area – better because it is remote – will cost about $3,000, including the charter of an air-craft to get into the headquarters camp. Some big game meat is wasted by trophy hunters but most resident hunters, who can get their game closer to home, shoot for meat as well as sport. Thousands of household freezers holding haunches of venison, moose and game birds attest to their prowess. Indians may hunt and fish all year, as may all resident deer hunters on the Queen Charlottes where a small species of deer threatens to overrun the Islands.

Golf is played all year on the coast. Victoria holds an annual Christmas Tree tournament on Boxing Day. When the TV production "Wonderful World of Golf" chose Capilano Golf Club in West Vancouver for one of its 1964 feature matches, host-pro Gene Sarazen said he regarded the course as one of the continent's top ten. It is considered as one of Canada's first three. Banff and Jasper are the others. One of the nation's most attractive is the Victoria Golf Club whose water hazards are the Pacific Ocean. From Prince Rupert, where the terrain would make a course too costly, devotees drive 80 miles to Terrace over a twisting road, play 36 holes and drive back the same day.

Tennis too is played on the coast all year except for February and March. Stanley Park's public courts are usually full on Christmas Day. Cricket has its followers. Swimmers pack the beaches in summer and there is the hardy Polar Bear Club which insists on dunking en masse in English Bay on New Year's Day. Curling is perhaps the fastest-growing sport. Moderate-fee, family-type clubs catering to curling have sprung up all over the province. Some have added skating, swimming pools and tennis courts as well. Rockhounding has some 9,000 adherents who search for jade and other rare rocks among the mountain creeks for their home tumbling and polishing machines. Beachcombing for the flotsam of the sea is an enjoyable and less arduous pastime. Riding the open range of a dude ranch, or as it is called now, a guest ranch, provides the annual holiday for many.

For campers, the government maintains 11 major provincial parks, laced with nature trails and preserved in their virgin state. In addition, there are nearly 100 well-planned campsites, mostly free, strategically placed for holidayers. Most are full by late afternoon from June to early September. There are also four national parks serviced by the federal government. For Vancouverites and Victorians there are the magnificent gifts of Stanley Park and Beacon Hill Park. Stanley Park, fast becoming too small for the thousands which pack it on fine weekends, opened in 1966 what is considered one of the continent's finest salt water aquariums.

The night attractions and restaurants of Vancouver encourage some to say the city is becoming the San Francisco of the north. The better restaurants have learned that décor and staging must be added to good food and patrons have become adventurous in their choice of wine and new dishes. The symphony orchestras of Vancouver and Victoria hold successful seasons. The playhouses of Vancouver and Victoria perform to ever-larger audiences. The Queen Elizabeth Theatre in Vancouver is busy with touring companies all winter; in summer with the Vancouver Festival. The Vancouver Opera Association stages five costly productions a year and provided Joan Sutherland with her world debut in *Norma*. There are many semi-professional "little theatre" groups and the university theatres are always active with experimental plays and films.

And when all else pales, there is the western sunset as it reddens the Pacific!

THIS IS THE SCENE, any sunny summer weekend, looking west from Fisherman's Cove, West Vancouver, Canada's largest marina. Sail boats of the West Vancouver Yacht Club are returning from a morning's racing event just off the entrance to Howe Sound.

The Impact of the Good Life

The booming economy of the mid-sixties has been felt throughout every walk of life in British Columbia. With more money to spend and more time to spend it, people everywhere have chosen some form of leisure activity. Some have two or three. The following photographs, taken the length and breadth of the province, depict only a few of the ways the British Columbian is enjoying his new-found affluence and the impact his land's resources have had on his life. With such temptations beckoning him it is a miracle he gets any work done at all. That he does is due, perhaps, to the creative and physical energy that seems to suffuse him. In any case, he has succumbed to the temptations and in his surrender he has found fulfillment.

OFF CAMPBELL RIVER an eastern visitor lands an 18-pound salmon on a Lucky Louie plug and with the expert assistance of fishing guide Mike Rippingale.

AT WESTWOOD TRACK (left) near Port Coquitlam in the Fraser Valley, sports-car racing continues all summer. Thousands have now become avid weekly spectators.

MOUNTAINEERING party plots attack on Mount Fairweather, at 15,300 feet the highest point in B.C. This is the northwest corner where province joins Alaska.

JADE HUNTER Ronald Purvis of Lillooet has turned a rock-hound hobby into a business. Each year he ships tons of green jade to Hong Kong and western Europe.

FALL FAIRS are held in almost every rural area the province over. This is the Agassiz Fair in the Fraser Valley when Dirk Van der Wyck became Corn King.

HUSBAND AND WIFE BIG GAME TROPHY HUNTERS, outfitted with Winchester Magnums and 4X scopes, watch California bighorn sheep near Ashcroft in early fall.

QUEEN ELIZABETH THEATRE PATRONS, Vancouver, throng the outdoor plaza during an intermission. This, with Playhouse beyond, forms enviable cultural complex.

SKIING IN BRITISH COLUMBIA is a choice between crowded weekend slopes and lonesome solitude that is never far from lodgings. This is Tod Mountain, Kamloops.

TO GARDEN (right) even on a moist morning when the mountains are shrouded in clouds, is to find satisfaction in solitude and tranquillity in serene calm.

VANCOUVER NIGHT SPOTS feature big-name headliners; have become favourite try-out centres for acts about to open long-run engagements on the Las Vegas strip.

GOLF becomes more than a game in British Columbia when it is played amid uplifting scenery that surrounds most of the province's year-round courses.

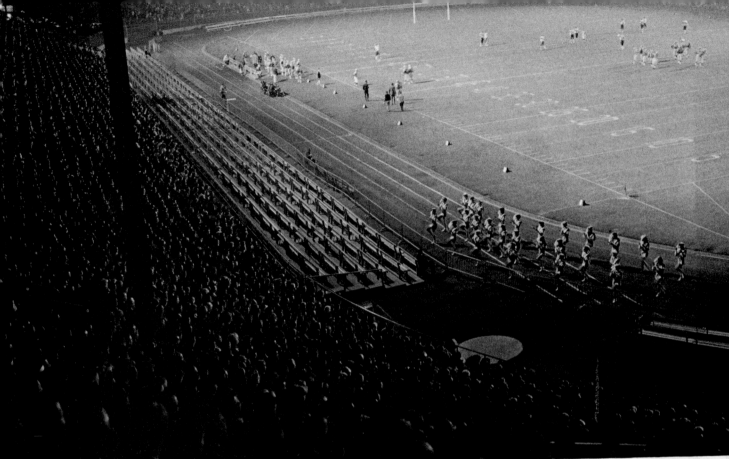

FOOTBALL at night in Empire Stadium has become traditional with Vancouver's B.C. Lions fans who average 31,400 per game for Canada's largest gate.

115 AIR MILES AWAY from the crowded scene above, a beachcomber, alone in thought, watches the Pacific rollers wash a beach of Vancouver Island's west coast.

SHOPPING has become less a utilitarian function and more a social activity with the advent of fine shopping centres all over the province. They offer a good selection of quality merchandise. Here at Kitimat, Alcan workers chat in the tranquil 9 p.m. twilight.

WILLIAMS LAKE STAMPEDE, in its 40th year, is Canada's largest annual stampede after Calgary's. The Dominion Day weekend meeting attracts many thousands.

GUEST RANCH RIDERS mount their trail-ride horses in a Cariboo corral for a morning in the saddle through the birch and willow stands of the big grass country.

TENTS, CAMPER TRUCKS AND TRAILERS are to be found in government campsites all over the province. This site is on the shore of Okanagan Lake near Penticton.

SALT-WATER SWIMMING in English Bay, Vancouver, has attained a new background with its bay-facing facade of new apartment buildings. There are also tidal swimming pools.

POOLSIDE LIVING, no longer considered a status symbol, permits swimming any time. Heated pools extend the swimming time into seven months between April and November.

DINING OUT has become a pleasurable and adventurous experience in a lot of specialty restaurants. Many feature the foods and customs of exotic countries on the Pacific rim.

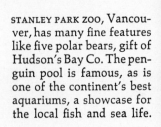

STANLEY PARK ZOO, Vancouver, has many fine features like five polar bears, gift of Hudson's Bay Co. The penguin pool is famous, as is one of the continent's best aquariums, a showcase for the local fish and sea life.

STANLEY PARK CHILDREN'S RAILROAD, over a mile long, carries a million passengers yearly and is only one of many children's attractions in 600-acre natural park.

BEACON HILL PARK, Victoria, (right) has become a marriage of old and new with the many apartments that have been erected on its perimeter. Nevertheless the park is still a haven for the city's senior citizens, the duck watchers, the Sunday painters, the flower lovers, the sunshine strollers, the horizon gazers on the cliff-side benches who follow the ships outward bound over the Pacific's horizon.

13

Reaching for Maturity

In terms of world history, world governments, world industry and world stature, British Columbia has just come of age. As it begins its second century it has only just begun to show its potential. It was a late starter but it has sprinted hard to catch up. Now without breaking stride it is settling into a long-distance endurance run. A measure of its pace is the official forecast that by 1973 spectacular gains will be made in all sectors of the economy: tourist revenues to $400 million; provincial ferry traffic up 84 percent; mining, petroleum and natural gas production up 74 percent; school enrollment up 34 percent; health and welfare expenditures up 70 percent. All these are projected on 1966 conditions.

When the year 2000 comes, a scant 34 years away, the province will be one third into its second century. Government leaders, industrial magnates, engineers and teachers who guided British Columbia to the threshold of its new greatness will have passed on. Children who began secondary school in the mid-sixties will be middle-aged. The population will exceed six million. The old speculation as to whether the pendulum of effort would shift from east to west may well have been decided. Possibly there will exist a Pacific Common Market of California, Oregon, Washington and British Columbia, quite dependent on each other's resources. The provincial gross product, estimated at $6 billion in 1966, will have risen to a conservative $140 billion based on the 10 percent annual growth rate during the sixties. For practical reasons, Canada may well be a nation of five regions – Maritimes, Quebec, Ontario, Prairies and British Columbia. Automation will be the benevolent monarch of the masses, with more employed to program, compute and service its machinery than ever were displaced by it. No man will be unskilled. Every professional will return to school a month a year to keep abreast of developments. The three-day weekend will be universal.

Dr. Gordon Shrum, chairman of the British Columbia Hydro and Power Authority, chancellor of Simon Fraser University, former professor of physics, says: "Whether British Columbians provide any leadership for the world's billions of people will depend upon our ability to remodel our educational system to keep pace with our technological advances. Education will have to change from being a single-shot at the beginning of our lives to a lifelong, everyday activity. Specific skills or bits of knowledge are no longer an important part of a child's early education because they are going to change very rapidly . . . We must adopt new methods, new objectives, new curricula and new philosophies."

Dr. Shrum sees the 21st century bringing instantaneous communication in three-dimensional colour video between individuals any place on earth, with automatic translation "a few cents extra."

In 2000, research will be the high altar of the forest products industry. Every ounce of effluent discharged into seas and rivers or released as air pollution in the sixties, will be captured and converted to add by-product dollars to the economy. Just as research now turns coal into nylon and aspirin, great industrial and government-backed laboratories will find a thousand uses for wood cellulose, ranging from foods to medicines, and the provincial forests will have attained world recognition as a prime source. Lumber will still be produced for structural timbers but other wood products like siding, panelling and dressed trims will be produced in stable dimensions and solid colours.

A woodsman of long experience, J. V. Christensen, president of the Tahsis Company Ltd., believes that logs will be carried in troughs on an airstream to a machine 20 meters long – he predicts a conversion to the metric system by 2000 – in which they will be sliced across the grain with one pass in less than a second into ultra-thin discs. The next machine will break up the discs and separate the bark. Then the chip stream will divide, one part going to the paper division, the other to building materials. In the latter, after cooking, and adding binding resins derived from the wheat-cleaning process, colour will be added. The homogenized, coloured pulp will be extruded to form only five standard sizes: three for structural uses and two for siding. Builders will cut this material with a high-frequency sonic saw. They will fasten the pieces together with a sonic fuser to create a welded joint. The interior wall panels will have built-in electric heating elements and will be fused to the structural members of the building. They will not rot, expand or shrink and will never need painting if the owner doesn't change his mind about the colour. Mr. Christensen predicts that tree fallers will use high-speed, air-driven saws operated from small compressors, with cutting speeds six times faster than gasoline-driven chain saws. Thin, synthetic-fibre ropes will replace thick steel cables to allow longer reaches and smaller winch drum diameters. Logging roads will only be subgraded because hovercraft will move 50 tons of logs to the mill in one fly-over. Retro-fire will reduce their downhill speed. Helium balloons may be used to lift logs from the steeper slopes. Like Dr. Shrum, Mr. Christensen emphasizes the role of education: "Eighty percent of future forestry crews will be graduates of a government technical forestry college," he says, "and it will be compulsory for all graduates to return to the college for a month a year if they are to keep their certificates in good standing." He believes the forestry work-year will be only eight months by then, leaving one month for the refresher course and three months for vacation.

W. D. H. Gardiner, western district general manager of the Royal Bank of Canada, agrees with him. "There will be far more leisure to enjoy the British Columbia outdoors," he says, "and by that time employers and employees will have learned to live and work together more co-operatively." Mr. Gardiner sees great industries located near the power sources of the Peace and Columbia rivers, conservation an even more integral part of the forest industry, more cattle raised in the interior, fish scientifically harvested by using sonar and undersea television. He continues: "Despite the fact the province will be Canada's California and reaping the benefits of thousands of ambitious people who will migrate here, our industries will still be suffering because of the added cost of transporting produce to the continent's greater markets which will still be located in the east and south. There will of course be the vast populations of China and other Pacific rim countries needing our products to meet the demands of their emerging peoples. One can envision artificial barriers having largely been removed insofar as exporting is concerned."

On banking, Mr. Gardiner predicts that by the year 2000, society will use no cheques and not much paper money. Only one credit card will be carried, he forecasts, to be inserted into a store's machine. Pushing a button to show the kind and amount of the sale will transmit the data to a master control centre which will electronically check the purchaser's branch bank for his credit status. That information will be relayed back to the store instantly.

Award-winning Vancouver architect, Arthur C. Erickson, concerned with urban development and land conservation, thinks it will be at least 2000 before a major change of attitude about British Columbia's cities, mainly Vancouver, brings a better use of land. "Civilization begins with conservation," he says. "The cities one loves are those receiving the greatest devotion from their people. This is so of San Francisco but it has not been so of Vancouver. Vancouver has been exploited for gain, not pleasure. When the turn of the century comes, the city's beauty will either have been destroyed or, if planning prevails, it will have grown exceptionally. By then, I hope, we will be giving it our time, endowing it with our money and enriching it with our dedication. By then the 330 miles from Vancouver to Portland will probably be one long, continuous city, a megalopolis, and the Pacific will be the new Mediterranean."

Abundant challenge in a land of abundant resources and abundant opportunity

...this is British Columbia, 100 years old

it speeds the road into its second century

The text of this book
is set in Palatino type.
It was printed and
bound in Canada
at the Evergreen Press,
Vancouver, British Columbia

Back end paper:
Bear River,
north of Stewart